KAUAI

AND THE PARK COUNTRY OF HAWAII

I have visited, a great many years ago, the Sandwich Islands—that peaceful land, that beautiful land, that far off home of profound repose, and soft indolence, and dreamy solitude, where life is one long slumberless Sabbath, the climate one long delicious summer day, and the good that die experience no change, for they but fall asleep in one heaven and wake up in another . . .

when you are in that blessed retreat, you are safe from the turmoil of life; you drowse your days away in a long deep dream of peace; the past is a forgotten thing, the present is heaven, the future you leave to take care of itself. You are in the center of the Pacific Ocean; you are miles from the world; as far as you can see, on any hand, the crested billows wall the horizon, and beyond this barrier the wide universe is but a foreign land to you, and barren of interest.

in place of the dingy horrors of the "Willows," and the painful sharp-pointed shrubbery of that funny caricature of nature which they call "South Park," I saw huge-bodied, wide-spreading forest trees, with strange names and stranger appearance—trees that cast a shadow like a thundercloud, and were able to stand alone without being tied to green poles . . .

Kukui trees, Awaawapuhi Valley

In those islands the cats haven't any tails, and the snakes haven't any teeth; and what is still more irregular, the man that loses a game gets the pot. And as to dress, the native women all wear a single garment, but the men don't. No, the men don't wear anything at all, they hate display; when they even wear a smile they think they are overdressed. Speaking of birds, the only bird there that has ornamental feathers has only two, just barely enough to squeeze through with, and they are under its wings instead of on top of its head, where, of course, they ought to be to do any good.

The native language is soft and liquid and flexible, and in every way efficient and satisfactory—till you get mad; then, there you are; there isn't anything in it to swear with. Good judges all say it is the best Sunday language there is; but then all the other six days in the week it just hangs idle on your hands; it isn't any good for business, and you can't work a telephone with it. Many a time the attention of the missionaries has been called to this defect, and they are always promising they are going to fix it; but no, they go fooling along and fooling along, and nothing is done.

It is a paradise for an indolent man. If a man is rich he can live expensively, and his grandeur will be respected as in other parts of the earth; if he is poor he can herd with the natives and live on next to nothing; he can sun himself all day long under the palm trees, and be no more troubled by his conscience than a butterfly would.

instead of that wretched cobblestone pavement nuisance I walked on a firm foundation of coral, built up from the bottom of the sea by the absurd but persevering insect of that name . . .

instead of the combined stenches of Sacramento Street, chinadom, and Brannan street slaughterhouses, I breathed the balmy fragrance of jessamine, oleander, and the Pride of India; in place of the hurry and bustle and noisy confusion of San Francisco, I moved in the midst of a summer calm as tranquil as dawn in the Garden of Eden: in place of our familiar skirting sand hills and the placid bay, I saw on one side a framework of tall, precipitous mountains close at hand, clad in refreshing green, and cleft by deep, cool, chasmlike valleys . . .

No alien land in all the world has any deep strong charm for me but that one, no other land could so longingly and so beseechingly haunt me, sleeping and waking, through half a lifetime, as that one has done. Other things leave me, but it abides; other things change, but it remains the same. For me its balmy airs are always blowing, its summer seas flashing in the sun; the pulsing of its surfbeat is in my ear; I can see its garlanded crags, its leaping cascades, its plumy palms drowsing by the shore, its remote summits floating like islands above the cloud rack; I can feel the spirit of its woodland solitudes, I can hear the plash of its brooks; in my nostrils still lives the breath of flowers that perished twenty years ago.

—MARK TWAIN

KAUAI

and the

Edited By Kenneth Brower

With a foreword by David Brower

Park Country of Hawaii

By ROBERT WENKAM

SIERRA CLUB · SAN FRANCISCO

*To my children, for whom I hope
there will always be wilderness to enjoy.*

Publisher's note: The book is set in Centaur and Arrighi by Mackenzie &
Harris, Inc., San Francisco. The color was lithographed by Barnes Press, New
York City. The paper is Champion Kromekote, double-spread collated and
bound in Columbia Mills' Sampson linen by Russell-Rutter Company, Inc.,
New York City. The design is by David Brower.

We are grateful for permission to reprint excerpts from these books:
Holt, Rinehart and Winston, New York: *God's Own Junkyard*, by Peter Blake,
    copyright 1964 by Peter Blake.
Alfred A. Knopf, Inc., New York: *Science in the Cause of Man*, by Gerard Piel,
    copyright 1961.
Random House, Inc., New York: *Hawaii*, by James A. Michener, copyright
    1959.
Random House, Inc., New York: *The Immense Journey*, by Loren Eiseley,
    copyright 1957.
The University of Chicago Press, Chicago: *The Kumulipo*, by Martha Beck-
    with, copyright 1951.

The Sierra Club, founded in 1892 by John Muir, has devoted itself to the
study and protection of national scenic resources, particularly those of mountain regions. All Sierra Club publications are part of the nonprofit effort the
club carries on as a public trust. The club is affiliated with the International
Union for Conservation, the Natural Resources Council of America, and the
Federation of Western Outdoor Clubs. There are chapters in California, the
Pacific Northwest, the Great Basin, the Southwest, the Great Lakes region,
and on the Atlantic seaboard. Participation is invited in the program to enjoy
and preserve wilderness, wildlife, forests, and streams. Main office: Mills
Tower, San Francisco. Other offices: The Biltmore, New York; 705 Dupont
Circle Building, Washington, D.C.; Los Angeles; Albuquerque; Seattle.

Contents

Photographs

Acknowledgments

In researching the history of Kauai for a book on its land I found much written about what people did *on* the land, but little about what happened *to* the land. Political histories and historical novels on Hawaii are abundant, but none of them told me why the islands we see today are so very unlike the islands Captain Cook saw.

I went to government file cabinets, read family correspondence, and waded through water-soaked monthly reports rescued by the State Archives from a flash flood in the state office building. I found all the Kauai territorial parks correspondence in the bottom of an old Del Monte pineapple carton. Each bit of history that I uncovered was a discovery for me, and I was entirely caught up in the search for more. I had not known that Hawaiians were afraid of the forest or that they had no real conservation tradition until I researched old manuscripts. I did not know that state personnel had themselves opposed radar installation in Kokee State Park until I found their interoffice correspondence, buried deep in the files.

Jim Ferry, chairman and member of the Board of Land and Natural Resources, granted permission for me to search the files of the State land office, and the files of the departments of Forestry, Fish and Game, and Parks. These government files were particularly valuable in supplying facts on the land management policies of the monarchy, republic, territory, and state. Amfac corporation spent a full day searching early records of Kekaha Sugar Company so that my chronological history would be in order. Miss Agnes Conrad, in charge of the State Archives, also rendered invaluable assistance in locating old reports and official correspondence.

Of the people who participated in the making of the book, probably the most helpful has been a camping companion of many years and an active member of the Windward Volunteer Rescue Squad, Richard Davis. Dick sometimes carried more than fifty pounds of my camera gear on his back, helping me into wilderness back country and moving me up precipitous palis with rope and piton. On one occasion, we were both lost in Alakai Swamp and struggled out two days later chased by hunting dogs.

The man who first suggested that I set down on paper my thoughts on Hawaiian conservation is a familiar name to all who are working to keep Hawaii beautiful. I first met Alfred Preis, architect, as his employee and worked for a year as designer in his Honolulu office—a period I'm sure he remembers as more talking than drafting. Fred's concern about man's relation to his environment has become an important concern in my own life.

Many kamaaina residents of Kauai graciously granted interviews and I heard from them bits of Kauai's history I could not have known otherwise. Especially helpful were Mr. and Mrs. Hector Moir, who greeted me with generous hospitality at their Poipu residence and directed me to numerous sources of information and out-of-print publications.

I want to thank the many people who offered inspiration and encouragement in my years of working with conservation organizations and community groups to save Diamond Head and the green hillsides back of Honolulu. I want to thank those who helped in the recent fight to prevent the destruction of Salt Lake by filling, and in the continuing fight to preserve the few remaining historical buildings in the islands.

I owe much to Dorothy Lindley; Wayne Collins; Nancy Bannick; National Park Superintendent Glenn Bean; Bill Ward; the women of the Outdoor Circle; Secretary of the Interior Stewart Udall; Governor John A. Burns, who appointed me a member of the State Land Use Commission; and to Dave Brower, who seems to excel in visualizing publishing ventures others think impossible, and Ken Brower, who patiently helped make the impossible happen here.

If "Requiem for Makapuu" saddened the public of Hawaii with its lament for natural beauty lost, perhaps this book can awaken the public everywhere to the beauty that can still be saved on Kauai, in one of the finest national parks of all.

R.W.

KAUAI

PACIFIC OCEAN

NA PALI

KE'E BEACH
HAENA BEACH

Waimha

LUMAHAI

Hanalei

NATIONAL GUARD
RADAR

PROPOSED KAWAIKOI
DAM AND RESERVOIR

MAKAHA
RADAR

MAKAHA RIDGE

NASA
TRACKING
STATIONS Halemanu

Kokee

NA PALI COAST

WAIALAE

BARKING SANDS

WAIMEA CANYON

SWAMP

Mana

OLOKELE CANYON

HANAPEPE VALLEY

Waiawa

Makaweli River

Kekaha

Waimea

KAUAI

NIIHAU

OAHU

Kalahe

MOLOKAI

LANAI

MAUI

Hanapepe

KAHOOLAWE

Hanapepe Bay

HAWAII

0   4 MILES

A much younger Hawaiian than I . . . explained that he was taught by his parents and grandparents that whenever the family went to the mountains for ti leaves for a small party, they would strip the ti leaves but leave the core of the plant to reproduce. If the leaves were for a large party, they would break off the leafy portion of the ti plant and plant a portion of the stock of the broken off piece of ti. This practice was necessary not only because the immediate family will again need the ti leaves, but also the neighbor, the other person, will need the life-giving ingredients of the ti plant.

The basic vestige of our heritage of being concerned for others is the inner human beauty that Captain Cook referred to when he described a populace with behavior patterns so free from reserve and suspicion which today we term, inarticulately, as our "aloha" spirit, a spirit of acceptance and concern for others.

In our present democratic society, we must bring people together in a closer relationship of concern for each other and thereby enhance . . . the ancient sense of the inner beauty of old Hawaii—a balanced relationship with nature.

—MYRON THOMPSON, *Chairman*
Land Use Commission, Hawaii

Foreword

Through the kindness of Robert Wenkam, I can write here as an expert on one subject—the overwhelming effect upon a man who loves the land of three days' exposure to Hawaii's natural beauty. Mr. Wenkam flew my wife and me all the way around Oahu, and also half way around Kauai. There we glimpsed the magnificence of what a Kauai National Park could encompass. We drove along a scenic highway, splendidly free of billboards and telephone wires, over to the windward side of that island and out to road's end at Napali, to feel the sea wind there and be amazed at the surf. With the car safely behind, we walked the first part of what must surely be one of the most spectacular trails on earth.

Repeatedly we had a chance to enjoy the only acceptable straight line in nature—the Pacific horizon from a beautifully situated spot on a Hawaiian island. It took me no time at all to understand why, at the turn of the century, my favorite uncle could have come to teach a semester of chemistry at Punahou—and be unable ever to leave the Islands. They named a building at Punahou in his memory. From my earliest recollections, I have loved Hawaii vicariously because of what he and his wife would tell me about it when, every other year or so they would trade their warm summer days for Berkeley's cool.

My brief look at Kauai and two days' exposure to Mr. Wenkam's devotion to its scenic resources provided the stimulus for what I said at a Governor's Conference on Natural Beauty held in Honolulu in February 1966, remarks that I borrow from in the paragraphs that follow, emboldened by the way

Hawaiians at the conference responded to them and because the whole complex of trip, people, and conference led to this book.

Governor Burns's conference in Hawaii was one of several state conferences on natural beauty that stemmed from the White House Conference of Natural Beauty in May 1965, a conference that itself grew from the earlier White House Conference of Governors called in 1908 by President Theodore Roosevelt, held soon after the word conservation was invented (the idea antedated the word by a good half century). The only voice for natural beauty at that conference came from the floor —J. Horace MacFarland's. His statement has been cited again and again, and most of the speakers on the program itself have been forgotten.

By the time the White House Conference on Conservation was called by President John F. Kennedy a remarkable change had taken place. As I remember it, all the speeches on the program were concerned in some way with the preservation of natural beauty, and the only strictly utilitarian speech, pleading for the usual orderly exploitation of commodity resources, came from the floor. I forget what the man said.

But we hear his speech often enough. Somehow in the course of it, whether the man favors logging something, or damming it, or digging it out or paving it, or eroding away its living soil, or adding pollutants to the air and water around it and junk to the landscape, he will profess that he too is a conservationist, a conservationist, mind you, who knows that conservation consists of wise use.

There, I allege, his creative thinking falters while he settles for his cliché. Nor has Webster done much better in defining conservation. His "wise use" definition will not serve our civilization well until we have a much clearer understanding of what wisdom consists of. The dollar doesn't measure it.

We haven't really been measuring any of our natural resources well because many of us have let a Conventional Wisdom get in the way of our thinking. We have settled for short-range predictions projected from a knife-edge instead of a base. Our perspective on what technology can do for us, and to us, is perilously limited. What man and technology have achieved is so spectacular that it preëmpts our attention; it lets us forget the most important element of all in what makes natural beauty something worth conferring about at the White House, in New York, in California, or in Hawaii.

That important element is life. The life force, the unbroken living chain that extends back to the beginning of life on earth, that from the long-ago beginning on down to each of us has never failed to reproduce itself well and move on. That force, in two billion years, also has produced a miraculous complexity of living things, each as dependent upon the others as a cell of one part of our body is dependent on those of its other parts. That life force has produced organic wholeness, and Robinson Jeffers would have us "love that, not man apart from that."

Do we? Or do we take that organic wholeness apart, tinkering with it and losing the parts, simplifying it without even asking how dangerous to us it may be to simplify it? Compulsively we take a natural piece of land, with all the species that magically convene on the surface we see, rising from below the surface out of all the life forms we can't see or know, and we order this miracle to reduce itself to a single crop. Instead of respecting the natural succession of cotton or cane, or peanuts or pine or tobacco, we simplify the biology without really knowing what we are doing to the land over the long run that man really must count on.

With our spanking new toy, technology, we have already done more to disrupt natural things in our own lifetimes than were disrupted by all the living things, including man, in all previous history. Whereupon, we freely predict that we can go on the way we're going, doubling our numbers every thirty or forty years, doubling our appetite for natural resources every decade, holding ourselves before the world as a model for all others, not thinking through, evading the truth that if the rest of the world obliterated resources at our speed, resources would go twenty times as fast as they are now disappearing. Can we go on this way, worship growth, confuse it with progress, and get on with it?

I don't think we ought to try it much longer. If we think we can get away with it because Science will save us, we haven't been listening carefully enough to the scientists wise enough to admit their own limitations. They, you, we, need to volunteer for the good war, the war against myth, the battle of words for the earth; we need to do the deeds that will rebuild the respect for the earth that our forbears had and our children might like a chance to discover.

Out of this effort a new understanding of conservation can come. We may see it not just a word to pay lip service to, or a dull thing that's no fun, or a shelf of books in the library talking about benefit-cost ratios and multiple use sweetened with Bambi, salted with Smokey—and who doesn't hate forest fires? We will see conservation instead as a starting point, wherever we may want to go; as an ethic; as conscience in our behavior toward our environment and all the living things that until now shared it with us—toward the life force that built into our own organism the ability to survive in our environment, and made that environment beautiful. The broad meaning of beauty will inform us.

When President Johnson called the White House Conference on Natural Beauty there was widespread concern about the limiting of the agenda. On May 23, 1965, the *New York Times* said that "the White House Conference on Natural Beauty . . . is slightly misnamed." The editorial went on:

"Since the emphasis of virtually all the planned panel discussions is on rectifying or at least concealing the ugliness which human beings have created in their environment, it might more properly be called a Conference on Man-Made Beauty. There is little or nothing on the agenda indicating concern about the national parks, the wilderness areas or the other great open spaces where natural beauty can still be enjoyed.

"From the program, one would never guess that there are sharp and bitter controversies now raging over proposals to build dams in the Grand Canyon, to drown millions of acres of Alaska by a huge dam project, to pollute the St. Croix River in Minnesota or to invade the primitive beauty of the Allagash River area in Maine, one of the last truly wild rivers in the eastern United States. A conference which apparently is going to ignore so many current struggles to preserve natural beauty in this country seems rather restricted in outlook.

"Within its own narrower frame of reference, however, it is still a conference very much worth holding. Human beings in this country, particularly in this industrialized, crowded century, have made a terrible mess of their urban and suburban landscapes. The conference intends to discuss the regulation of billboards, urban sprawl, landscaping of roads and parkways, control of auto graveyards and other junk heaps. Water and waterfronts, city parks and open spaces, and similar topics. Every one presents a problem in itself, and every one needs the public attention that this conference will focus upon it—an attention that is the first step toward improvement."

I believe that the Sierra Club membership of 47,000 agree with the editorial, and so would the forty other national organizations joined informally in the Natural Resources Council of America. Concern about what's happening to natural beauty, as opposed to man-made beauty, is becoming world-wide.

In California we are learning, and learning late, that a booming growth is no blessing at all. We would like very much to give back to New York the problem of being Number 1 in population. We suspect that New York doesn't want it back. The bigger its biggest city gets, the more buildings, the more throughways and cars, somehow the worse off the city is financially. Newspapers strike, subways strike, reservoirs go dry and lights go dark—all a result of growth that operates faster than man can organize for it. When this rampant growth happens in an individual we call it cancer. Come what may, out of some compulsion, we grow. Instead of growing to meet a need and then letting up, we just grow to grow. We are not far enough removed from the ruler who, when he died, ordained that his slaves must be killed and buried with him. It is not slaves that we would have lie with us in our graves, but something we have even less right to arrogate to extinction—the continuum of life that preceded man, and is entitled to survive him.

All of this was almost heresy a year or so ago. It isn't any more because we find that our own sins are being visited on us, with distressing swiftness in California. Raymond Dasmann's *The Destruction of California* says what I don't like to hear about my native state, but I know it's true. We grew too much. We've logged and smogged California; we're filling its finest bay so that we can build another Los Angeles in a state that deserves only one. We've mined its gold and now are mining its soil and air; our streams are being spoiled, our mimeographed subdivisions coalesce into slurbs, we have declared war on our terrain and our environment. There are many quick benefits for a few; there will be lasting deprivation for all others. Asserting leadership in an unhappy game, we have taken a fairly good creature, Man, who in the course of eons learned to stand upright, and have given him a smaller and smaller plot to stand on and hardly anywhere to walk on his own good feet; as fast as we can we are taking away even his visual rights, his chance to like what he seeks when he looks upon his horizon.

In a small way we are in the publishing business in the Sierra Club. Should we wait for events justifying a similar book— "The Destruction of Hawaii?" Or should we just publish this one, to talk about the preservation of Hawaii, of what people in the Islands have done and are doing to lead the overmature states back to a state of reason, to explain how Hawaiians want another generation to enjoy as they have enjoyed things that give their land its special meaning.

What way is Hawaii trending? What was Hawaii like in your own inventory of recollections? What was it like in the days you have read about? I have an old Christmas card that shows Diamond Head from Waikiki—and no work of man but a sailboat, an outrigger, and other men. As I look today at the buildings jammed up against what was once so beautiful a crater I am reminded of arriving passengers at the airport awaiting their baggage and so crowded up against the carousel or railing that no one can see his baggage. If each would step back a little and take his turn, all could see.

Looking at Diamond Head, we might review how fast the change has been, and consider what will happen if this same rate of change is extended on into the future, this same urge to grow and double-grow, ever multiplying what man can super-

impose upon this land and always dividing what God left here. How boldly can we revise our thinking? How big our plan to survive our own cleverness? How creative can the genius in each of us be—the genius that is the really crucial resource—in our learning not to live alone, but to grant other life forms the right to coexist?

"Not blind opposition to progress," the Sierra Club says in a slogan, "but opposition to blind progress." Progress is a new concept, man-made, endowed with no special virtue beyond what man attributes to it. Man has a capability of looking ahead. Our own predictions can be as accurate as we want them to be. Can they be big enough to include, while there is still time, an assurance that Hawaii will remain uniquely beautiful? Can Hawaii's plans include, for all the states and for the world as well, a generously spacious Kauai National Park? I earnestly hope so. The Sierra Club would like to do everything it can to help this come about, using as well as we can what seventy-five years have taught us about how vital national parks can be for everyone. In each of the main parks on the coast, Yosemite, Sequoia, Kings Canyon, and Olympic, we have seen the most intense and violent local opposition at the outset become strong support for the park *after* it was established.

The national parks, the national wilderness system, the wildlife refuges—these have been a best foot put forward by that part of America administered by the United States. They exemplify what we can do when we sense that man has other talents than the talent to disrupt the land organism, when we remember that the life force we save is not our own, but a force that made us possible and that is essential, in its wonderful complexity, to our staying aboard the planet. The parks prove that we are bright enough to show restraint, to set aside what we cannot replace. Hawaii's parklands—with Kauai National Park an integral part—will help spread around the world a special appreciation of goal expressed by Adlai Stevenson not long ago. "We travel together," he said, "passengers on a little space ship, dependent on its vulnerable reserves of air and soil; all committed for our safety to its security and peace; preserved from annihilation only by the care, the work and, I will say, the love we give our fragile craft."

In their own way, the Hawaiian Islands are fragile craft. The world knows that they have been easy to love. So they have been. So they can be. But only if man lets them.

DAVID BROWER
Executive Director, Sierra Club

Honolulu, February 3, 1966
(adapted at 35,000 feet, westbound, February 17 and 25, 1967)

NOTE: For what has been done here to help the world keep up its love for Hawaii, we share Mr. Wenkam's gratitude to all the people, in and out of the sugar industry, who made this book possible. I myself am grateful above all to Mr. Wenkam, a most perceptive author and photographer, and Kenneth Brower, whose sense of editing and design is sure, and a delight, too. His comments about Mr Wenkam, the book, and the place stem from his having spent some time with all three last fall:

"Robert Wenkam has much in common with Valdemar Knudsen, the early planter whose story he tells here. Though their arrivals were a century apart, both men fell in love with Hawaii and adopted the islands as home. Their love was not the love typical of newcomers to Hawaii; they were not much enamoured of the rich soil and what it might produce, or of the pleasant climate, or of the beaches. They were not excited by the potential of Hawaii, but by what Hawaii was—by the land itself and what was native to it. The two ranged their adopted country widely, a century apart, the earlier arrival on his horse, the later on his very long legs.

"Both Wenkam and Knudsen arrived as young men, unsure of the direction their lives would take. For both, the Hawaiian land made the decision—a healthy way to have one's destiny shaped. Knudsen became a sometimes farmer and Hawaiian chief. Wenkam became a photographer and a conservationist, the leader of the fight for a national park on Kauai.

"To make the photographs for this book Robert Wenkam had to change his style. Before, he had worked professionally as an advertising photographer and had specialized in photographing architecture; now he had to photograph the absence of architecture, or architecture of other-than-human origin. It wasn't easy—it's hard for a man six feet eight inches tall to photograph lichens and other things growing close to the ground—but this book marks his success. His dedication to the park idea drove him, and he surprised himself. Not a scholar, he learned research, and inexperienced at writing, he learned to write. It was an exemplary adaptation, the kind of thing that happens when a real commitment motivates a man.

"The country of western Kauai would make a unique national park. Its forests are like no other forests in our national park system, and its sea cliffs like no other cliffs. There are birds and plants there found nowhere else, last Hawaiian examples of the local modification that makes islands so interesting to evolutionists. Best of all, there are the *Menehune*, the tiny forest men who came to Hawaii before the Polynesians and are still in the deep forest, according to Hawaiians who should know. (Recently a class on Kauai was disrupted when one of the children saw a Menehune by a well. The teacher joined in the hunt, which continued until the principal arrived.)

"No present national park boasts supernatural beings, not Yellowstone nor Yosemite nor Grand Canyon. Here, then, is the chance for a truly unique national park, and Wenkam saw it—the opportunity to make an invaluable addition to our nearly perfect park system."

D.B.

26

Genesis

Lines from a Hawaiian creation chant

At the time when the earth became hot
At the time when the heavens turned about
At the time when the sun was darkened
To cause the moon to shine
The time of the rise of the Pleiades
The slime, this was the source of the earth
The source of the darkness that made darkness
The source of the night that made night
The intense darkness, the deep darkness
Darkness of the sun, darkness of the night
   Nothing but night

     . . .

The night gave birth
Born was Kumulipo in the night, a male
Born was Po'ele in the night, a female
Born was the coral polyp, born was the coral, came forth
Born was the grub that digs and heaps up the earth,
    came forth
Born was his child an earthworm, came forth
Born was the starfish, his child the small starfish
    came forth
Born was the sea cucumber, his child the small sea
    cucumber came forth
Born was the sea urchin, the sea urchin tribe
Born was the short-spiked sea urchin, came forth
Born was the smooth sea urchin, his child the long-
    spiked came forth
Born was the ring-shaped sea urchin, his child the
    thin-spiked came forth
Born was the barnacle, his child the pearl oyster came
    forth
Born was the mother-of-pearl, his child the oyster
    came forth
Born was the mussel, his child the hermit crab came
    forth
Born was the big limpet, his child the small limpet
    came forth
Born was the cowry, his child the small cowry
    came forth
Born was the naka shellfish, the rock oyster his
    child came forth
Born was the drupa shellfish, his child the bitter
    white shellfish came forth
Born was the conch shell, his child the small conch
    shell came forth
Born was the nerita shellfish, the sand-burrowing
    shellfish his child came forth
Born was the fresh-water shellfish, his child the small
    fresh-water shellfish came forth

Out from the slime come rootlets
Out from the slime comes young growth
Out from the slime come branching leaves
Out from the slime comes outgrowth

Born was man for the narrow stream, the woman for the broad stream
Born was the ekaha moss living in the sea
Guarded by the ekahakaha fern living on land
Darkness slips into light
Earth and water are the food of the plant
The god enters, man cannot enter
Man for the narrow stream, woman for the broad stream
Born was the tough sea-grass living in the sea
Guarded by the tough land-grass living on land

Man for the narrow stream, woman for the broad stream
Born is the Nanana [sea spider] living in the sea
Guarded by the Nonanona living on land

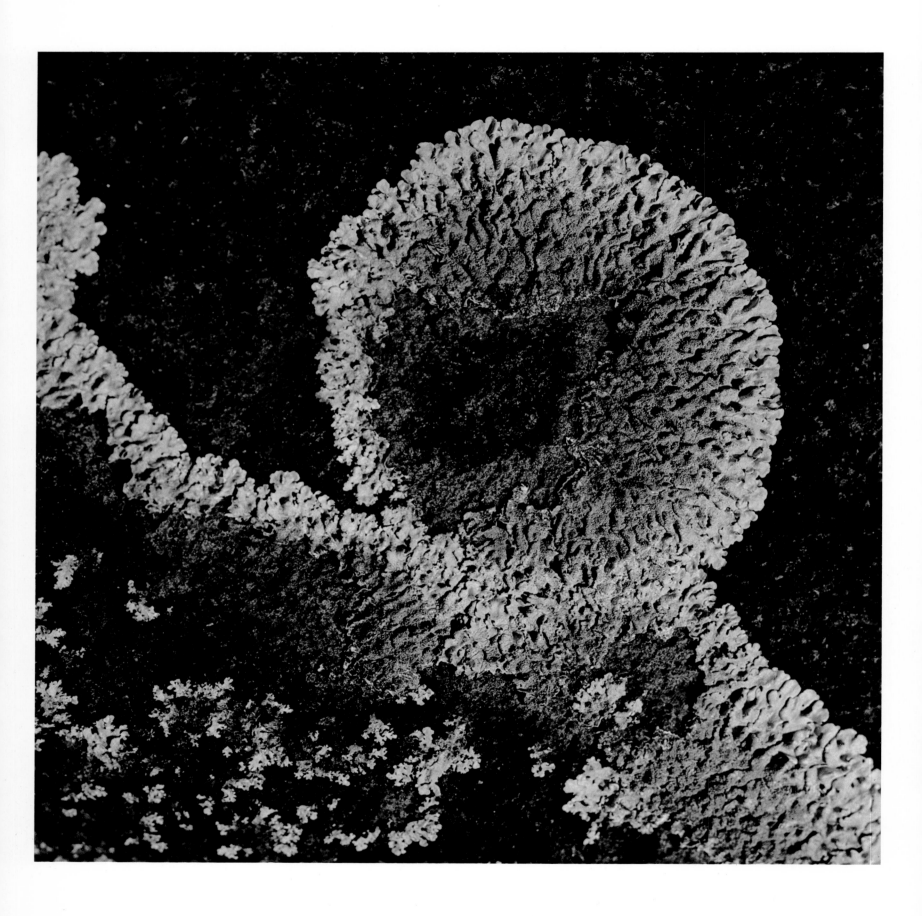

Darkness slips into light
Earth and water are the food of the plant . . .
Water that caused the withered vine to flourish
Causes the plant to develop freely
Multiplying in the passing time
The long night slips along
Fruitful, very fruitful
Spreading here, spreading there
Spreading this way, spreading that way
Propping up earth, holding up the sky
The time passes, this night of Kumulipo
    Still it is night

Born was the egg, the parent
Out came its child a bird, and flew
Born was the Snipe, the parent
Out came its child a Plover, and flew
Born was the A'o bird, the parent
Out came its child an A'u bird, and flew
Born was the Turnstone, the parent
Out came its child a Fly-catcher, and flew
Born was the Mudhen, the parent
Out came its child an Apapane bird, and flew
Born was the Crow, the parent
Out came its child an Alawi bird, and flew
Born was the 'E'ea bird, the parent
Out came its child an Alaaiaha bird, and flew
Born was the Mamo honey-sucker, the parent
Out came its child an 'O'o bird, and flew
Born was the Rail, the parent
Out came its child a brown Albatross, and flew
Born was the Akikiki creeper, the parent
Out came its child an Ukihi bird, and flew
Born was the Curlew, the parent
Out came its child a Stilt, and flew
Born was the Frigate bird, the parent
Out came its child a Tropic bird, and flew
Born was the migrating gray-backed Tern, the parent
Out came its child a red-tailed Tropic-bird, and flew

Born was the Unana bird, the parent
Its offspring the Heron came out and flew
   Flew hither in flocks
   On the seashore in ranks
   Settled down and covered the beach . . .

Land birds were born
Sea birds were born
Man born for the narrow stream, woman for the broad stream
Born was the Stingray, living in the sea
Guarded by the Stormy-petrel living on land

Man for the narrow stream, woman for the broad stream
Born was the Sea-swallow, living at sea
Guarded by the Hawk living on land

Nothing but darkness that
Nothing but darkness this
Darkness alone for Po'ele'ele
Still! it is night

North ridge, Hanakapiai Valley

The night gives birth to prolific ones
The night is swollen with plump creatures
The night gives birth to rough-backed turtles
The night produces horn-billed turtles
The night gives birth to dark-red turtles
The night is pregnant with the small lobster
The night gives birth to sluggish-moving geckos
Slippery is the night with sleek-skinned geckos
The night gives birth to clinging creatures
The night proclaims rough ones
The night gives birth to deliberate creatures
The night shrinks from the ineffective
The night gives birth to sharp-nosed creatures
Hollowed is the night for great fat ones
The night gives birth to mud dwellers
The night lingers for track leavers
Born is the male for the narrow stream, the female for the
    broad stream
Born is the turtle [Honu] living in the sea
Guarded by the Maile seedling [Kuhonua] living on land

Ohia seedlings, Kokee

Man for the narrow stream, woman for the broad stream
Born is the sea-borer [Wili] living in the sea
Guarded by the Wiliwili tree living on land

Man for the narrow stream, woman for the broad stream
Born is the sea-worm living in the sea
Guarded by the bastard sandalwood living on land

Man for the narrow stream, woman for the broad stream
Born is the Okea living in the sea
Guarded by the Ahakea tree living on land

Man for the narrow stream, woman for the broad stream
Born is the sea-urchin [Wana] living in the sea
Guarded by the thorny Wanawana plant living on land

Man for the narrow stream, woman for the broad stream
Born is the Nene shellfish living in the sea
Guarded by the Manene grass living on land

Man for the narrow stream, woman for the broad stream
Born is the Liko living in the sea
Guarded by the Piko tree living on land

Man for the narrow stream, woman for the broad stream
Born is the Opeope jellyfish living in the sea
Guarded by the Oheohe [bamboo] living on land

Man for the narrow stream, woman for the broad stream
Born is the Nanana [sea spider] living in the sea
Guarded by the Nonanona living on land

Born was Pola'a
Born was rough weather, born the current
Born the booming of the sea, the breaking of foam
Born the roaring, advancing, and receding of waves,
    the rumbling sound, the earthquake
The sea rages, rises over the beach
Rises silently to the inhabited places
Rises gradually up over the land

Born is the stormy night
Born the night of plenty . . .
Dead is the current sweeping in from the navel of the
  earth: that was a warrior wave
Many who came vanished, lost in the passing night

Born were men by the hundreds
Born was man for the narrow stream
Born was woman for the broad stream
Born the night of the gods
Men stood together
Men slept together
They two slept together in the time long ago
Wave after wave of men moving in company . . .
Tranquil was the time when men multiplied
Calm like the time when men came from afar
It was called Calmness [La'ila'i] then
Born was La'ila'i a woman
Born was Ki'i a man
Born was Kane a god . . .

Born was Kanaloa the hot-striking octopus . . .
Born was Creeping-ti-plant [La'i'olo] to man
Born was Expected-day [Kapopo], a female
Born was Midnight [Po'ele-i], born First-light [Po'ele-a]
Opening-wide [Wehi-loa] was their youngest
These were those who gave birth
The little ones, the older ones
Ever increasing in number
Man spread abroad, man was here now
    It was Day

The Kumulipo
—translated by MARTHA BECKWITH

THIS IS the story of Hawaii, told in the history of its land. Specifically, it is the story of the Ahupuaas—the districts—of Kekaha and Waimea, on Kauai, the land probably first seen by Tahitians from double-hulled ocean canoes on their first voyage to the islands they would call Hawaii; the land first seen by Captain Cook on his search for a northwest passage; the first large land area leased by a king of Hawaii; a land planted in sugar cane, ravaged by wild cattle, designated in part as forest reserve and proclaimed Hawaii's first major state park.

The story is a cry of pain, for the land has been hurt. It has been trampled harshly since Captain Cook stepped ashore almost two hundred years ago. The fragile balance between man and environment has been seriously disturbed by man's use and exploitation of the island of Kauai.

This is the story of wise land management, and laissez-faire enterprise for individual wealth; of primitive communal rights, and sophisticated zoning laws; of careful planning of man's environment for long-term benefits, and government manipulation for political gain. It is the story of an island and of how man has encroached on it, irresistibly and persistently; the story of man's failure at individual, voluntary custodianship of land that should be held in trust for future generations.

1. Discovery

Toward the end of the eighteenth century Hawaii was discovered for the second time in nine hundred years. The first discovery, by Polynesians, had changed the land little, but the second discovery was by a different sort of man.

IN THE winter of 1777-78, Captain James Cook sailed north from Christmas Island for five weeks, searching for a northwest passage. On February 1, he wrote in his log: "The wind shifted, and a storm came on, preceded by a lowering darkness, that prefaced some violent convulsion, and soon after it broke forth in thunder, lightening, wind, and rain, which in two hours increased to such a raging degree, as no man on board had ever known the like. Fortunately, it was but of short con-tinuance; but, in that little time, the sea broke over our quarter, and cleared the decks of everything that was loose. After this we had a gentle breeze a east and east southeast which continued till we arrive in the latitude of 7 deg. 45 min. north and in 205 deg. east longitude, where we had one day of perfect calm. A northeast by east wind then succeeded, which blew faintly at first, but freshened as we proceeded northward. We daily observed tropic birds, boobies, etc. and between the latitude of 10 and 11 deg. north we saw several turtles. Though all these are considered as signs of the proximity of land, we discovered none till early in the morning of Sunday, the 18th, when an island appeared bearing northeast by east not long after more land was seen, which bore north and was totally detached from the former. At noon, the first was supposed to be 8 or 9 leagues distant. Our longitude at this time, was 200 deg. 41 min. east and our latitude 21 deg. 12 min. north. The next day, at sunrise, the island first seen bore east distant 7 leagues, not being able to reach this, we shaped our course for the other; and soon after, observed a third island, bearing west northwest. We had now a fine breeze at east by north and, at noon, the second island . . . for the east end of which we were steering, was about two leagues distant. As we made a nearer approach, many of the inhabitants put off from the shore in their canoes, and very readily came alongside the ships."

Captain Cook put ashore at Waimea and looked from the sea to the wooded mountains of this strange land he named in honor of the Earl of Sandwich. He noted only "grass tuffs, not even shrubs," where he landed. The lower part of the country was treeless. He saw few coconuts, only a rare breadfruit, and "houses scattered about without any order."

Cook compared Hawaii unfavorably with Tahiti, but found on Kauai "a greater quantity of gently-rising land, [which] renders it, in some measure, superior to the above favourite islands, as being more capable of development."

For seven years after Cook's departure, no foreigner set foot on Kauai, until Captain Vancouver came. Vancouver presented to a Waimea Chief the first sheep and horned cattle ever seen in the islands. He also gave to one of the chiefs "some vine and orange plants, some almonds, and an assortment of garden seeds."

The discovery of the islands of Hawaii opened up new lands for foreign businessmen, who sailed from Europe and America. Fortune-hunters joined conservative financiers in acquiring land on all the islands—legally or otherwise. The Hawaiian civilization was corrupted by American business in an era of great disappointment to frustrated missionaries. King Kalakaua, in a poker game, showed the mood of the times. The King, playing with Maui sugar baron Claus Spreckels, said, "I have five kings," placing on the felt table top his hand of four kings and pointing to himself as the fifth.

The Monarchy's objective of increasing the Islands' export revenues led to the support of a single-use land policy and a plantation system of efficient land utilization. Little attempt was made to encourage homesteading or to establish family farms. Most of the valuable lands suitable for large-scale agriculture, much of the beach land, and the desirable urban areas were quickly acquired through widespread grants to large plantations and private estates. With few exceptions, most of the public lands were marginal acreage: swamplands, eroded pasture, and inaccessible mountain lands.

The Hawaiian native population was dropping alarmingly and land was plentiful. Mark Twain visited Hawaii and reported: "The natives of the islands number only about 50,000 and the whites about 3,000, chiefly Americans. According to Capt. Cook, the natives numbered 400,000 less than a hundred years ago. But the traders brought labor and fancy diseases—in other words, long, deliberate, infallible destruction; and the missionaries brought the means of grace and got them ready. So the two forces are working along harmoniously, and anybody who knows anything about figures can tell you exactly when the last Kanaka will be in Abraham's bosom and his islands in the hands of the whites. It is the same as calculating an eclipse—if you get started right, you cannot miss it. For nearly a century the natives have been keeping up a ratio of about three births to five deaths, and you can see what that must result in. No doubt in fifty years a Kanaka will be a curiosity in his own land, and as an investment will be superior to a circus."

The few remaining forests diminished as great sugar plantations spread across the land. A koa tree at that time, as an investment, would have been superior to a circus—except that no one was interested in seeing a koa, and certainly not in paying admission.

Forests receded, and the barren fields of dry, red earth at Makaweli fed giant dust clouds. Red dust, carried by trade winds, blew miles out to sea at Waimea and Kehaha. For days at a time during trade-wind weather, ships could not see the harbor and were forced to wait offshore.

The land was changing, but industry was prospering. In a few decades Hawaii was to boast the largest sugar plantation, the largest fruit farm (pineapples), and the second largest cattle ranch in the United States.

2. Alii O Kauai

The Eden the Hawaiians had known was transformed.
Sugar became the most important force in the islands, and its
cultivation had an unparalleled impact on the Hawaiian
landscape. The industry had slow and difficult beginnings,
dependent upon the dedication of the pioneer planters,
men who worked hard, risked much, and often lost.

VALDEMAR KNUDSEN arrived in Hawaii in April, 1854, from California's Feather River country, with little experience in ranching or agriculture. He took an early liking to the warm west shore beyond Waimea, and gratefully took up the offer of his friend, ranch-owner H. A. Widemann, to tend several dozen head of cattle. Knudsen was able to fatten the cattle quickly on the warm Kekaha grasslands, and acquired valuable experience in ranching operations. The aggressive and sensitive young bachelor quickly adopted Hawaii as home, learned the Hawaiian language, and soon gained the friendship and confidence of both native chiefs and commoners.

A contemporary of Knudsen, Archibald Archer, was the first white farmer of Kekaha. He grew oranges, coffee, and tobacco in Hanalei Valley, and cleared ground for tobacco in Mana. Hoping for better growing weather, Archer sought and was granted the first Crown lease in west Kauai, yet continued to plant in Hanalei, hiking there across the vast wet top of Kauai in two days, following old Hawaiian trails. He built a small grass hut at Halemanu to rest overnight on his incredible journeys up Mana Ridge on horseback, across Alakai Swamp to Kilohana on foot, and down the almost vertical palis of Wainiha Valley. After holding the lease for five years, he lost everything following an extended drought. Then his partner died. Discouraged, he sailed away after reaching an agreement to have Knudsen take over the lease.

Knudsen negotiated a new thirty-year lease with King Kamehameha's commissioners of public lands. For an annual rental of four thousand dollars in U.S. gold coin, he signed the lease for all commercial rights to "those tracts of land situated at Waimea, island of Kauai, Hawaiian Islands, known as the Ahupuaas of Kekaha, Pokii, Waiawa, Mokihana, Milolii, Nualolo, and Mana, by their ancient boundaries . . . subject however to the legal rights of native tenants."

In addition to the usual lease conditions and clauses covering reversion of improvements to the kingdom, the Crown's in-denture included a new lease condition reflecting concern by the King over the depredation of his forests for sandalwood and the increasing damage from wild cattle. The lessee was admonished not to "permit or suffer to be done, any willful or voluntary waste, spoil or destruction . . . upon the above demised premises, or cut down, or permit to be cut down any timber trees now growing or which shall hereafter grow . . ."

Knudsen built his home at Waiawa on the edge of Mana Swamp. At that time the great swamp covered large areas of the lowlands and its connected brackish lakes allowed natives from Mana Village to paddle on an inland sea as far as Waimea. Migratory ducks flying the Pacific on their southern route fed on the swamp plants. Thousands of Hawaiian stilts stood on spindly pink legs in the still swamp waters. Dunes rippled along the coral limestone shoreline and protected the lakes from high seas and salt water.

The high plateau behind Knudsen's home was blanketed by a dense and luxuriant forest of indigenous ohia lehua, and koa. The abundant birds, of varieties he had never seen before, Knudsen carefully collected and sent to Washington. One skin—that of the cranelike Hawaiian stilt—was new to the Smithsonian Institution scientists, who named the bird after its finder: *Himamtopus himamptopus Knudseni*. The Hawaiians simply called it Aeo.

When Knudsen signed the Waimea lease, he became a konohiki, or chief, by appointment of Kamehameha IV. In this office he possessed princely powers over a district that covered more than one hundred square miles—almost all the west side of Kauai from the sandy shore at Mana to the high Waineke pond of Kokee and beyond to Napali.

Hundreds of natives were scattered through the district, living in grass huts and tending taro patches that had been in continuous use since ancient days. Knudsen spoke to them in Hawaiian and received their loyalty. They called him Kanuka. He was the *Alii O Kauai*, the Lord of Kauai.

Knudsen lived in a time of bold transition; transition from ancient native tenancy to modern leasehold, from the absolute powers of the Konohiki to those of the landlord.

Before Knudsen's coming, in 1840, the new constitutional monarchy had proclaimed revised labor-tax laws as a first step in reforming the feudal kingdom of King Kamehameha. The new laws provided that the commoner would no longer be required to work for the king and chiefs on every week of the month: "the first week of the month the people shall work two days for the king and one for the landlords, the second week in the month they shall work one day for his Majesty, the King, and two days for the landlords, and the next two weeks the people shall have to themselves."

The annual royal tax was in accordance with a regular system, assessed on the smallest divisions of land, and was paid somewhat as follows: one *ili* (individual parcel) was "taxed a hog, a dog, a fish net, a fish line, a cluster of feathers, and 20 *kapas* [tapa cloths]." Some of the kapas were to be nearly square, for bed clothes, and some narrow and long for women's dresses.

The new laws also provided for a redistribution of the fishing grounds. Waters outside of coral reefs were assigned to the commoner; those between reefs and beach, to landlords. Certain specified grounds and species of fish were "placed under the protective tabu of the tax officers for the king." Sandalwood trees, the oo and mamo birds, and "all large trees such as one cannot clasp" were tabu, and violation was punished by a fine of "one hundred rafters each five yards long." The beach was unassigned and available to all. To this day, the beach between the high water mark and the sea remains reserved for public use.

The foundation for the Monarchy's land reform had been laid long before. By the time Captain Cook arrived on Kauai, the Hawaiians had already established land divisions on the separate islands for easier control and tax collecting. Each island was divided into districts called "mokus." The large moku was divided into long pie-shaped parcels that extended from the mountains to the sea, and were called "ahupuaa." Managed by konohikis, these unique land divisions enabled commoners living on the ahupuaa within their chief's authority to satisfy the tax collector without trespassing on ahupuaas of adjacent chiefs. Fish and seaweed were obtained from the sea; taro, bananas, and sweet potatoes from the lowlands; and feathers, canoe logs, and spears from the mountains. Ahupuaas varied greatly in size and were sometimes cut off from access to the sea or mountains by the odd shapes of other ahupuaas, but their primary purpose of providing for all a man's needs was an unusual characteristic for a political land division.

Smaller units within the ahupuaas were *ili*, each with its own name and carefully defined boundary. Sometimes an *ili* was divided and its parts separated. The natives called this kind of ili a *lele*, the Hawaiian word for jump.

The cultivated portions of the ili were subdivided further into small tracts of land called *moos* or *mooainas*. Occasionally a moo was subdivided again into smaller parcels called *paukas*. The commoners facilitated tax payments by cultivating still smaller plots which were worked on the "chief's day." Since these patches were generally worked only on Friday, they became known as *poalimas*, Fridays. The native's own small farming patch, which he tilled for himself and his family, was called a *kihapai*.

The single most important land reform by the Hawaiian Monarchy was the Great Mahele—the Great Division—of 1848. Its proclamation by King Kamehameha III opened the way for private ownership of land. In the Great Mahele the land interests of the king and high-ranking chiefs were divided among the people in a momentous undertaking of far-reaching consequences.

In 1845, a Land Commission had been appointed by King Kamehameha III to determine the rights of all individuals to their claim in the land, whether they were chiefs or commoners. The Land Commission, in carrying out its work, had recommended division of all lands into three parts: the king's personal property, the land of the chiefs and konohikis, and the land being tenanted by the common people. The Mahele made no provision for ownership of land by the tenant Hawaiians, although a bill of rights did protect them from unwarranted dispossession.

The king and chiefs strongly objected to the idea of distributing their land, but they yielded to pressure from the sugar planters and the realization that the economy of the islands would suffer unless the old feudal system was abandoned. More than two hundred and forty of the highest ranking chiefs and konohikis participated. The individual divisions were recorded in a huge book called the "Mahele book," with lands signed over to the chiefs listed on the right side and lands reserved for the king on the left. The Mahele was made without any survey, the land being identified by its ancient name and described in the Mahele book by natural geographic features, a mountain ridge or the bottom of a gulch, and sometimes merely by a field of grass, the stone walls of taro patches, or a particularly large and significant tree. The descriptions of early land divisions still plague surveyors, and many carefully described parcels are today unlocatable.

The King's personal properties were called The Crown Lands, and the lands of the chiefs and people were called Government Lands. Government Lands were leased or sold from time to time as a means of obtaining revenue to meet the increasingly high costs of the government and to satisfy the demands of the sugar planters and ranchers for large landholdings.

As the king and chiefs began to dispose of their newly acquired holdings, many questions arose regarding the rights of native tenants. To clarify the situation, the privy council authorized the land commission to award fee simple titles to all native tenants without payment, finally allowing the commoner to own his own land. These parcels of various shapes and sizes became known as "Kuleana Lands" and today are proudly owned by the few Hawaiians still living on the land.

It was necessary for the native tenant to file legal claims for his kuleana, but many thousands failed to register or to appear before the Land Commission in support of their claims. Of the approximately 4,000,000 acres of land divided in the Great Mahele of 1848, only 30,000 acres of land were awarded to native Hawaiian commoners; however, these were mostly taro lands, at the time considered the most valuable lands in the islands.

Few Hawaiians understood the new land laws, and the isolated natives of Niihau Island were not alone in failing to register the land their fathers and ancestors had lived on for generations. On Niihau only one parcel was recorded with the king's appointed registrars.

Niihau was one of several grants of land offered to the Sinclair family by King Kamehameha V. The island stood across the channel from Waimea, fifteen miles from Kauai. Francis Sinclair, who liked the idea of owning his own island, convinced the family of Niihau's potential as a ranch, and in 1864 they paid the king ten thousand dollars for sole ownership. The family moved to Niihau, where they immediately found their newly purchased authority as landlords challenged by the native Hawaiians, who had no understanding or respect for private land ownership. The land had always been theirs to grow crops on and hunt as they needed to feed and clothe their families. Their only obligation had been to the Hawaiian chiefs who received a share of the yams and an occasional pig.

Sinclair's revival of the old feudal rental system and his refusal to recognize Hawaiian ownership of kuleanas the Hawaiians had neglected to legalize generated ill will among the Hawaiians and destroyed the Sinclairs' dream of an island paradise. Sinclair demanded one or more day's labor a month in exchange for rights to live and hunt on Niihau. Many natives refused to comply and few had any desire to hire out as ranch hands. Fish were plentiful in the sea and taro was easily available from Kauai. Sweet potatoes and yams grew alongside their grass huts and coconuts loaded the palms overhead. Working for the Sinclair family appeared to offer nothing they did not already have in abundance.

Ranching operations virtually stopped when one elderly Hawaiian couple refused to allow cowboys to graze cattle across their kuleana or even to set foot upon the land they claimed for their own. The disputed strip of land reached from the mountains to the sea, and cut off all travel from one end of the island to the other. The Sinclairs were dumbfounded when proof was offered that 50 acres of land on Niihau had indeed been granted to an Hawaiian named Papapa by King Kamehameha III in 1855, nine years before the Sinclairs' purchase. The king in selling Niihau apparently overlooked the earlier grant, and the new owners were now challenged by two hostile Hawaiians who refused to allow them even a right-of-way across the narrow parcel.

Francis Sinclair discussed his problem with Valdemar Knudsen, konohiki of western Kauai. Sinclair was willing to pay one thousand dollars for the land, though the entire island had sold for only ten thousand. Knudsen was held in high respect by the Hawaiians in his ahupuaa. He agreed to negotiate with the Papapa couple and asked Sinclair to bring him one thousand silver dollars.

Arriving on Niihau by longboat, Knudsen traveled overland on horseback to the Papapa's grass hut on the western shore, and introduced himself. As he talked with the old couple, he carefully stacked the silver dollars in orderly rows across the lauhala mat spread over the floor. The old man kept shaking his head "no," emphasizing again and again his unwillingness to sell. Knudsen continued to stack the silver coins, telling the couple

of the new merchants on Kauai, where the land was gentler and greener, and where they could enjoy their remaining days without ever working again. The piles of coins, ten to a stack, grew on the mat. The old man repeated no, as his wife's eyes opened wide in wonder. She listened silently. At last Knudsen shrugged and began unstacking the coins. Suddenly, the wife uttered an ancient Hawaiian exclamation, "Schah!," reached out, and pulled the treasure into her lap. The Sinclairs at last owned all Niihau.

The Sinclairs soon became aware that Niihau was useless as a profitable ranch, and purchased Makaweli grant, probably the most valuable single parcel on Kauai, stretching from Waimea River to Olokele and Hanapepe, from Waialeale to the sea. By 1957 the family's lands on Kauai and Niihau totaled 97,291 acres with an estimated market value of $4,971,000. Niihau's 46,000 acres were worth only $190,000.

As pioneering traders and merchants began to seek fortunes in cattle and sugar, the problems experienced by the Sinclairs on Niihau became commonplace across the land. Communications with the king were very unreliable, and it was not in the best interests of the chiefs to proclaim the new rights granted to the commoners in a way that all would understand.

Valdemar Knudsen escaped much of this trouble. He understood the Hawaiians and was almost as undemanding as they were in his relationship with the land. He was a poor businessman and an undedicated farmer. He experimented freely with his land, importing plants from many countries. Visiting botanists from all over the world were his house guests, and many responded to his hospitality with gifts of fruit and flower seeds. Knudsen's Waiawa property blossomed with trees and vines from far lands. He brought in the first kiawe tree seeds to Kauai from Honolulu's Catholic mission; his cattle were to fatten contentedly on the ripe seed pods in later years during the long, hot Kekaha summers. The swamps with his beloved birds remained undisturbed, and he urged the king to protect Nohili, Kawalele, and Kolo ponds at Mana as game preserves.

When Knudsen and Dora Isenberg, wife of the German manager of Lihue Plantation, received packets of koa haole seeds, Knudsen planted his near Waiawa, from where they soon spread to all sections of the island. The koa haole plants provided excellent cattle feed, but were to become an unsightly pest. Dora Isenberg remarked later that "You can blame Valdemar for koa haole—I flushed mine down the sink!" Winds blew the flat brown seed everywhere.

Knudsen ranged far and wide on his favorite horse, Pukuniahi, planting orange trees in every gulch piercing the Mana Pali, where they grew rapidly and flourished. When the bachelor Knudsen courted and received the hand of Annie Sinclair, he gathered his own orange blossoms and carried the fragrant bouquet to his bride. They settled down quietly to live on his adopted land.

Captain Christian L'Orange, a sailor who left his ship in Honolulu to make a fortune on the land, formed a partnership with Knudsen. They planted the first commercial sugar cane in the Kekaha area at Pokii in 1878. Knudsen improved the small spring at Kauhika with a steam pump and hired natives at fifty cents a day to plant cane and harvest the crop. When the

Hawaiians tired of working for wages and went fishing, the partners sold out to two other planters who were willing to take over.

Knudsen returned to his ranch, boiled down wild cattle for tallow, bailed hides, and sold salted meat to whalers. The high mountain country provided ideal pasturage for breeding the bullocks that hauled the large bull-carts, piled high with hand-cut sugar cane, to the new cane-grinding mill at Kekaha. Paying the annual land rental proved difficult until Knudsen's subleases for sugar cane began earning a regular income. Knudsen was often forced to pay the rental with taro, firewood, breadfruit, and pigs brought to him by the natives on his orders as the konohiki of Waimea.

It was a frontier life for the Knudsens. Henry Restarick, the Bishop of Honolulu, visited the family when they were well established at Waiawa, and later described his trip and the life there.

I was to be the guest of the Knudsens at Kekaha, and I shall never forget the ride from Eleele to their home. It was before the great improvement was made in the roads and the red dust was deep, impalpable and penetrating. A bath with three changes of water did not eliminate it from the pores of my skin, or my hair, and my hosts, the Knudsens, laughed when, like David Harum, I apologized for the state of the towels. They comforted me by saying that when I reached home my pillows would show for weeks where I had been. I have since heard the story of the Kauai man who made a journey round the world, and on reaching San Francisco, on his way home, he took a Turkish bath. When he was rubbed down the man said, "you are from Kauai, sir." "How do you know?" "I can tell from the color of the dirt. I was there once myself."

Knudsen's nephew from Norway, Hans P. Faye, joined the small group of cane planters in later years. It was he who drilled the first artesian well near Waiawa. Cane grew rapidly in the warm sunshine and plentiful water, attracting new investors and planters from all sections of Kauai. A Chinese merchant, Pah On, built a rice mill at Waimea and harvested rice at Mana in quantities sufficient to supply all the islands until the Sacramento delta was planted, making his venture unprofitable in competition with cheaper California rice.

The Hawaiians could not be persuaded to work on the plantations, and it became necessary to import Portuguese, Chinese, and Japanese as contract laborers. Discouraged by what he felt was the failure of his Hawaiians, and aging, Knudsen became seriously ill from a recurring fever and disappeared for months at a time, leaving Annie to care for the children and manage the lands, with help from her brother Frank on Niihau. Paul Isenberg convinced Annie that she should sign over all the sugar-growing lands to a new planters' company he organized, which would harvest the cane and divide the profits between themselves and Annie. She agreed, keeping their home at Waiawa and the grazing land above the Mana Pali. The new sugar firm, Kekaha Sugar Company, prospered and paid Annie's share of profits in raw sugar, bagged and warehoused in her name.

In July 1918, Knudsen's sons, Eric and Augustus, upon advice that the sugar enterprise was a risky business, sold the remaining term of Valdemar Knudsen's lease to Kekaha Sugar Company. Eighteen months remained of the thirty-year lease that was paying Annie eighty thousand dollars a year for government land leasing at four thousand. Fortunes were handsomely made in sugar and Kekaha was no exception.

Valdemar Knudsen died in Honolulu in 1898. He had helped plant the seeds of a growing industry with powerful political influence, an industry that history credits with overthrowing the monarchy and bringing about annexation of Hawaii to the United States. As the sugar industry prospered, the Hawaiian culture dwindled, and the vigor and glory of the race disappeared. The native grass-hut villages and taro patches were replaced by a new civilization and land wrapped in a green carpet of sugar.

WHY WE SHOULD ANNEX

Now, let us annex the islands. Think how we could build up that whaling trade! Let us annex. We could make sugar enough there to supply all America, perhaps, and the prices would be very easy with the duties removed. And then we would have such a fine half-way house for our Pacific-plying ships; and such a convenient supply depot and such a commanding sentry-box for an armed squadron; and we could raise cotton and coffee there and make it pay pretty well, with the duties off and capital easier to get at. And then we would own the mightiest volcano on earth—Kilauea! Barnum could run it—he understands fires now. Let us annex, by all means. We could pacify Prince Bill and other nobles easily enough—put them on a reservation. Nothing pleases a savage like a reservation—a reservation where he has his annual hoes, and Bibles and blankets to trade for powder and whisky—a sweet Arcadian retreat fenced in with soldiers. By annexing, we would get all those 50,000 natives cheap as dirt, with their morals and other diseases thrown in. No expense for education—they are already educated; no need to convert them—they are already converted; no expense to clothe them—for obvious reasons.

We *must* annex those people. We can afflict them with our wise and beneficent governments. We can introduce the novelty of thieves, all the way up from street-car pickpockets to municipal robbers and Government defaulters, and show them how amusing it is to arrest them and try them and then turn them loose—some for cash and some for "political influence." We can make them ashamed of their simple and primitive justice. . . . We can give them juries composed entirely of the most simple and charming leatherheads. We can give them railway corporations who will buy their Legislature like old clothes, and run over their best citizens and complain of the corpses for smearing their unpleasant juices on the track. We can let them have Connolly; we can loan them Sweeny; we can furnish them some Jay Goulds who will do away with their old-time notion that stealing is not respectable. We can confer Woodhull and Claflin on them. And George Francis Train. We can give them lecturers! I will go myself.

We can make that little bunch of sleepy islands the hottest corner on earth, and array it in the moral splendor of our high and holy civilization. Annexation is what the poor islanders need. "Shall we to men benighted, the lamp of life deny?"

—MARK TWAIN

Hartford, Jan. 6, 1873.

3. Sugar

*Sugar interests dominated island politics and their right
to do as they pleased with the land was unquestioned. No voice
spoke for the integrity of the land, and the land suffered.*

THE COURSE of public land use following the Great Mahele is well illustrated in the history of lands occupied by Kauai's Kekaha Sugar Company. Kekaha's history is a part in the story of how a government-sponsored land monopoly determined not only the economy of the islands, but also the very mood and appearance of the land.

Outright purchase of large land grants by the plantations had been stopped long before Kekaha Sugar was founded. The Kingdom's policy of leasing lands instead of selling them had been initiated in order to halt the rapidly dwindling public domain. Later, the United States Congress, in writing the organic act establishing the Territory of Hawaii, included provisions that protected Hawaiians from being stripped of their land heritage, and the leasing policy was continued for that purpose.

Kekaha began its corporate history as the only plantation completely on government-leased land. Businessmen of the time must have raised their eyebrows as Kekaha cleared land, planted cane, and constructed a grinding mill at great cost, all with only a fifteen-year lease. The venture proved quite profitable, however.

As Kekaha's first lease renewal time approached, plantation manager Hans P. Faye became concerned when the new Territory of Hawaii asserted that upon termination of the lease expensive mill machinery would revert to the government, in addition to buildings, irrigation ditches, and other improvements. Faye disagreed with the Territory, and in a letter to C. T. Bailey, Commissioner of Public Lands, offered $150,000 to buy the land around mill and plantation improvements, pleading that he could not make needed mill improvements without full ownership. Without objecting Commissioner Bailey deleted the

40-acre mill site from Kekaha's 28,000-acre master lease, and following the provisions of the organic act, placed the land on the auction block for the competitive bidding that had to occur before land was leased. March 13, 1922 was the day of the auction. Only two Honolulu men registered to bid: W. T. Bottomley, acting as agent for Kekaha, and his close friend, E. White Sutton of Bishop Trust Company. The auction took only a few minutes. The short-term leases on pastures and rice fields went to Kekaha at the upset price (the fixed minimum price) of $3,000 annual rental. The fifteen-year sugar-land lease also went for the upset bid of $103,000 plus 7½ per cent of gross sugar receipts. Kekaha had no other bidder for its mill, so the Territory, having agreed that Faye's offer for the forty-acre mill site, camp lands, and improvements was fair and equitable, sold the mill outright to Kekaha in fee simple for $150,000 cash.

The ranch lands brought out curious competitive bidding. Sutton raised the $3,600 upset price by five dollars. Bottomley smiled and raised it another five. "Sold," said the Territorial land agent, and Kekaha acquired the ranch land lease for $3,610. Competitive bidding had occurred for the first and only time in Kekaha's history.

With factory improvements completed and secured by fee simple ownership of the mill site, manager Faye examined his company's leased acreage closely for new cane lands to feed greater tonnage into his modernized mill. Additional raw sugar could be produced profitably with little increase in overhead. Kekaha could also safely increase planting without fear of losing leasehold lands. Without the mill, Faye correctly reasoned, no one would ever be able to outbid Kekaha, which would obtain every future lease at the upset price. Faye's first move was to

gradually phase out the rice growers around the Mana ponds and to replant the paddies in cane.

On August 20, 1925, Faye wrote again to land commissioner Bailey and asked if Kekaha might be able to obtain on lease the Mana game reserves. The Territorial Division of Fish and Game said they "were not interested in creation of a reservation" at Mana, although at the time of the 1922 public auction the lands were specifically excluded from the lease and designated as a game reserve. Knudsen was no longer able to speak for his birds, and the plantation-oriented Territorial Land Department wrote Faye asking him to submit an offer for the 583 acres. This Faye did, and the only remaining migratory bird ponds on Kauai were leased at public auction to Kekaha Sugar for an annual rental of $900, the upset price.

Kekaha dispossessed the Hawaiian stilts, the migratory birds, and ducks from their native habitat. The ponds were filled and planted in cane. In 1936, Governor Lucius G. Pinkham's executive order setting aside 550 acres of Mana land for a territorial airport was also canceled. The airport pasture lands were leased to Kekaha, which promptly planted them in cane. The Territory's unwritten policy of promoting a single industry and a single land use was revealing itself as Kekaha expanded rapidly across all available land, eliminating the small farmer and showing little sympathy for conservation concepts encouraging protection of unique flora and fauna. Even Knudsen's old Waiawa home with its view across the Mana ponds to Niihau was dismantled, trees uprooted, and the yards planted in cane.

Chinese and Japanese contract laborers found it difficult to grow vegetables in backyard gardens in Kekaha because of the consistently hot weather, scanty rainfall, and sandy soil. During dry seasons the community was isolated and almost wholly dependent upon mainland importations shipped via Honolulu. Often the workers went without fresh vegetables for weeks at a time. Manager Lindsay Faye responded to their complaints, and 50 acres of marginal land above the mill became a truck-farm operation with all work done by hand. The operation was successful and soon expanded to 125 acres in a higher area at 2,500 feet, suitable for year-round vegetable growing, along the new Kekaha irrigation ditch bringing water from Alakai Swamp. No effort was made to sell outside the community, and Kekaha soon found itself the only company town in the Territory growing its own food and raising its own meat and poultry. Kekaha was entirely self-sufficient.

The second round of fifteen-year lease negotiations opened in 1936 with a letter from H. A. Walker, Honolulu financial agent for Kekaha Sugar Company, proposing new lease terms to the Land Commissioner, suggesting that the annual land rental be computed as a percentage of gross sugar proceeds.

When maverick Kauai Senator Charles A. Rice read Kekaha's proposal, he wrote the new Commissioner of Public Lands, L. M. Whitehouse, a letter that was to postpone the public auction and was perhaps the first direct challenge of Kekaha's land monopoly and long land tenure. The Senator wrote, in words that must have sounded heretical to the sugar planter communities of 1936, that "The proposition he makes is so unfair to the Government and taxpayers that I request before any action is taken that I be given an opportunity to appear before the Land

Board as a Senator from and one who knows the conditions at Kekaha."

Charles Rice ran his own political organization on Kauai and was subservient to no one. He was no longer general manager for American Factors on Kauai and he showed little inclination to recognize old loyalties. He stuck to his principles regarding the Kekaha lease. When Elsie Wilcox of Grove Farm opposed his continued chairmanship of the Senate Ways and Means Committee, Rice retaliated by selling private property in Lihue town to Kress Stores and a Japanese merchant, opening up the first competition to the American Factors' company store in Lihue. Before Rice's action, no merchant was able to buy land in Lihue because almost all the town was owned by Lihue Plantation.

The threat to Kekaha's tenure had been raised. Others would soon enter the arena to take the company on.

Fred Patterson, a young Honolulu attorney apparently representing a Los Angeles syndicate, was the first to step forward. He wrote Whitehouse that he wished to bid in the 1938 auction and requested that the Territory provide a new mill site on government land so he could bid competitively against Kekaha. He even offered to build a new mill if he submitted the highest bid. He asked further that a sealed confidential-bid procedure he followed so that Kekaha would be forced to bid higher than the upset price to give a fairer return to the government.

Kekaha had been a profitable enterprise during the old lease. Capital stock was doubled by the issuance of stock dividends amounting to $1,500,000, all of which was directly or indirectly earned from government-leased land. In addition, at the end of 1935 undivided profits totaled $1,422,813. During the thirteen years of the lease, average yearly cash dividends were $397,500 or 27.1 per cent on capital stock. The company had clearly profited beyond all reasonable expectations. The national depression did not affect Kekaha Plantation.

Water rights were publicly owned, as well as the irrigation ditches built by Kekaha Sugar. Without tremendous quantities of water, there would be no sugar—and no profit. Under these conditions it was reasonable to assume that there be a fair division of profits between the company and the Territory.

The Land Department had enough independence to suggest in a memo "that a fair and reasonable rent for the Kekaha lands would be an equitable division of the estimated profits"—a frightening proposal for the government to have made in the ultraconservative Hawaiian business community of 1936.

Early the next year, Senator Rice, who was now Chairman of the Territorial Senate Committee on Public Lands, wrote the assistant to Secretary of Interior Harold Ickes, complaining about the low rentals paid by the sugar plantations. He suggested that homesteaders would be willing to pay more. He wrote, "While I understand that not all of the government land leased to plantations can or should be cut up because of the irrigation and harvesting elements, I believe that at least 100 more of these homesteads could be disposed of on Kauai with a general good effect on the population." He gave as an example lands on eastern Kauai. Here the government lease on sugar lands had not been renewed, and instead had been divided into sixty-one three-acre lots for homesteading and sale at auction.

"As a result of this opportunity, citizens of the Territory now own their own lands and homes, with surrounding gardens. There was spirited bidding at the auction. More than forty of the lots brought more than the upset price."

The leasing of large blocks of government land at low cost to the sugar and ranching industries had long blocked the creation in Hawaii of an independent, farm-owning population, and was described by the 1937 Congressional Statehood Committee as "one of the outstanding evils of Hawaii's present economic setup." Senator Rice agreed.

It was at this time that Governor Joseph Poindexter received a concerned note from the U. S. Department of the Interior which said, "The decreased income to the Territory is undoubtedly causing an increase in the taxes paid by the people of Hawaii." The governor asked for an investigation. It had become obvious, even in Washington, that government land leases were being manipulated to keep the land available to only a favored few.

This high-level correspondence did not ruffle the Land Commissioner. His office was dedicated to furthering the best interests of Hawaii's fastest growing and most profitable industry. After receiving a letter from Kekaha stating they wanted payment made as originally requested—on a sliding-scale percentage of gross—and would have nothing to do with a division of net proceeds, he asked the Land Board to approve Kekaha's application for a new lease.

The lease application, prepared by C. T. Bailey, former Territorial Land Commissioner and new manager of American Factors' Land Department, was submitted to the Board in October, calling for a new lease at the upset minimum of $130,000 and sliding-scale payments at 7½ per cent of gross proceeds. The Board ignored Senator Rice's objections, unanimously approved the application, and moved for the auction to be held. As an added measure to make it more difficult for outside bids in the future, Board member Charles Hite, then also Secretary of Hawaii, moved that the power plant and campsite lands of the plantation be sold outright, although they were completely surrounded by Territorial lands. It was in this manner that Kekaha was to acquire in fee simple the powerhouse site deep in the bottom of Waimea Canyon. The legal requirements were met and the cards stacked against any outside bidders for the Kekaha lease.

Pan American's Trans-Pacific China Clipper service brought Hawaii suddenly closer to the mainland, with some new problems for the Land Commissioner. In the fall of 1937 businessman George Rodiek sent a personal letter by clipper mail from San Francisco to Secretary Charles Hite. Rodiek made a lease proposal "which, at all times, would give the landowner 50 per cent of the profits made by the operating company." Rodiek wanted to bid on cane land only, and made an offer on that basis. Whitehouse, apparently attempting to discourage any bidding from outside Hawaii, replied that the new lease rate would have to include all cane and ranch lands, 36,760 acres. This was the difficulty for outsiders anticipated by Bailey when he made his comprehensive bid application.

With the Patterson and Rodiek syndicates seriously interested in bidding, things were becoming complicated for Land Com-

missioner Whitehouse. Other problems came up. One day he opened a registered airmail letter from Kauai carried by the new interisland airways. It was from Henry K. Aki in Lihue, writing for a "blank application for homestead in the island of Kauai." Whitehouse was pleased to answer what he thought to be a routine request and directed Aki to D. F. Hurley, land agent in Lihue, who shortly informed Honolulu that Aki wanted many copies and would Whitehouse "please send us a supply."

Whitehouse wrote Hurley anxiously by return mail, asking what was going on over on Kauai and "What land, or lands, Henry Aki plans on having petitions filed?" The new airmail service brought a prompt reply. "Please be informed," wrote Hurley, "that he refers to the lease to the Kekaha Sugar Company . . . he said that he 'will see that the Hawaiians get a chance to own their own homes.'"

Now even the Hawaiians were after the Kekaha lands. Aki wrote Princess Kawananakoa, a member of the Hawaiian Homes Commission, regarding lands for the Hawaiians on the Mana and Kekaha uplands. These were Hawaiian Homes Lands, and Hawaiian homesteaders, by law, should receive first choice.

Territorial Land Commissioner Whitehouse expressed no concern for the Hawaiians or their rights to the land. In an amazingly unconciliatory letter to the Hawaiian Princess, he said that "since I have not received any notice from the Hawaiian Homes Commission that it is the intention of the Commission to select portions of the above mentioned lands for their use . . . it is the intention of this office to lease again these lands."

San Francisco's Rodiek wrote again in December renewing his lease proposal for the entire acreage, further proposing "that the cost of purchasing the present mill or the erection of a new plant, should be deducted from the lease rental . . . by doing this, the Territory of Hawaii would own the entire project with all operating factors at expiration of the lease." Whitehouse could, with ease, have expressed interest in this proposal, of obvious benefit to the Territory. His reply was simply, "law does not permit this."

In the morning mail of May 10, 1938 Governor Poindexter received a bulky envelope from Kauai. It contained a petition of twenty-five names, requesting "twenty acre homesteading lots for cultivation of sugar cane or other products" on Kekaha sugar and grazing lands.

Four hundred residents of Kauai were said to be ready to file, mostly farmers already skilled in sugar growing. They wanted their own farms and wished to move home and families onto the land, declaring this would not stop sugar production at Kekaha, but would result in independent farmers growing cane, which would be sold to the Kekaha Sugar mill for processing. The great water resources high in the Kokee mountains, owned entirely by the government, would make it an easy matter not only to grow sugar cane, but to permit the development of private diversified farming and a dairy industry as well. Kekaha Sugar had already proved the feasibility of the homesteaders' arguments by operating their own truck farm on the very same Hawaiian Homes land.

In the end, the threat from the homesteaders was met easily by the industry. The planters had simply to point to a provision they had written into the homesteading law, a provision that

excluded, from those Territory-owned lands available for home-steading, the lands leased to the sugar industry. Governor Poindexter, a Democratic appointee of President Franklin D. Roosevelt, stopped the homesteaders' plea for land by rejecting their petition. He backed up Whitehouse and members of the Board completely.

On June 8, 1938 the Kekaha lands were leased at public auction for the upset price of $130,000 to Kekaha Sugar Company. There were no other bidders.

World War II put a temporary end to the land debate. Kekaha was in full production, supplying sugar for the war effort. By 1942 Faye's upland plantation farms were producing more than 600,000 pounds of vegetables a year; clearly the land was suitable for truck farming, and Hawaiian farmers would have done well there. After supplying local markets, Kekaha sold surplus fresh produce to Kauai wholesalers in Lihue. Large quantities were also consumed by the Army and some even found their way to Honolulu. By 1943, 800,000 pounds of produce were being harvested, principally beans, corn, summer squash, cabbage, potatoes, tomatoes, carrots, rutabaga, lettuce, peas—almost anything that Faye could find seeds to plant.

At the end of World War II, Hal Hanna, Territorial Representative from Maui, reopened the land debate. Speaking before the Legislature, he stated, "Former Territorial Land Commissions literally gave thousands of acres of Hawaii's land leases to the big interests of the Territory for a mere song." He claimed that the Territory realized only $139,000 yearly for pasture lands and $290,000 yearly for sugar and pineapple lands, at the rate of only seven or eight dollars a year per acre. "Total revenue to the Territory from all land leases per year is only $1,247,891." Considering the large amount of government land under lease, Hanna concluded that "in a community as wealthy as Hawaii, somebody is getting away with something. The Territory receives too little."

The legislative flurry died quickly. While appointed Governor Ingram Stainback echoed Hanna's charges, Republicans representing sugar interests still controlled the majority vote and quietly pigeonholed in committee the bills introduced by Hanna. Not until statehood, fifteen years later, was any serious attempt made to revise Hawaii's public-land laws.

During the last days of the first political campaigns for state offices, Republican-appointed Governor William F. Quinn responded to the growing dissatisfaction of Hawaii's land-hungry residents and revived the plea Kauai's citizens had made two decades before. Quinn proposed a "second Mahele" and in a program designed to have wide popular appeal he suggested opening up large areas of public land on all the islands for sale. Included in his proposal were all of Kekaha Sugar Company's mauka cane and pasture lands. Undoubtedly guessing that the plan was nothing more than a political gambit and that the proposal would never be implemented, Kekaha refused to take the gubernatorial candidate seriously.

Hawaii was treated to the unusual spectacle of its Democrats opposing a land-reform program. They considered the Republican Mahele a great hoax, arguing that the bulk of the lands to be sold were already under long-term lease for sugar and cattle. They claimed that selling this land to individuals would "wreck the sugar industry" and "destroy the agricultural industry."

Quinn won the election, but failed to gain the backing of Kauai Senator Francis Ching, a Republican and the chairman of the Lands Committee, for legislation to put into effect a second Mahele.

Kekaha expanded its land-reclamation program even as the Legislature prepared to overhaul the public-land laws. An extensive drainage canal and pumping system was installed, capable of handling 80 million gallons a day for irrigation and pumping another 40 million gallons of swamp seepage into the sea. Sandy flatlands and drained lowlands were filled with bagasse, sugar-mill trash, and mud from cane washing equipment, then flooded with waste water to speed up decomposition in an organic land-recovery program. The new land was planted in cane or used for irrigated pasture and alfalfa. Intensive land use continued to be a major program at Kakaha in its efforts to increase land production to its maximum.

In the winter of 1953 Kekaha Sugar signed a new lease with the Territory of Hawaii for an upset annual rental of $201,608 for 28,021 acres. As usual, there were no other bidders for the lease, which would not expire until December 1968.

Fortune magazine once spoke of the system that keeps Hawaiian agriculture from collapsing in a competitive world as "paternalistic semi-feudalism." The system depends on control by a single industry over private and public lands. With statehood the system and the land laws that perpetuated it became obsolete. By common agreement among legislators, the 1961 regular session of the Legislature was to be a "land Legislature." It was to be, but it failed to pass a new land law, despite numerous extensions granted by the Governor for further meetings of the Senate-House Conference Committee, which was attempting to hammer out a compromise land law.

Liberal and conservative principals resisted compromise, and discussions bogged down completely on the question of the sale of public lands for commercial use. The basic stand of the new postwar Democrats was that the state should not sell its lands, while their Republican counterparts took the position that the State should do its utmost to promote economic development and that public lands should be made available, even for outright sale.

Democrat Representative David McClung stated that no large land leases should be granted in order that small-scale agricultural enterprises might have opportunity to develop. The sugar people quickly took particular issue with McClung. Kauai's Senator Ching said that a 500-acre lease limitation urged by McClung would threaten the operation of Kekaha Sugar Company. He asked if the Representative meant to force the plantation management to negotiate sixty separate leases from the Land Board and compete at public auction with countless other parties for the use of land on which its continued operation depended. The land committees were unable to resolve their differences.

The next Legislature, a year later, successfully compromised by agreeing that the final determination of land exchanges and sale of public lands for public use would be by legislative act. But the main body of Hawaii's land laws went unchanged and the political struggle over land reform would continue to be a major issue in future elections.

Political scientists Robert Horwitz and Norman Meller, in a review of Hawaii's land and politics, said:

The protagonists in this struggle had truly been "playing politics," but in a more basic sense than that term generally implies. The resolution of the land issue would, as they saw it, vitally affect the very character of Hawaii's regime, for the ownership, control, and utilization of her lands affect the quality of life of virtually every inhabitant of the Islands. The principles underlying the land issue were fundamental, for the protagonists rightly understood that while land laws of one sort are compatible with a plantation economy, extreme differences in wealth and status, and concentrated political power, land laws of another kind will promote the development of varied economic enterprises, more egalitarian division of wealth, and broader participation in government. The land issue in Hawaii has been—and will continue to be—linked inexorably with the extent to which the Islands' regime is more or less oligarchic, or more or less democratic.

Horwitz and Miller concluded:

So long as fundamental differences of opinion about the nature of the good life and the just society divide Hawaii's citizenry, the issue of "land and politics" will continue to be stoutly contested in Iolani Palace.

Canefield

4. The Forest

*The Hawaiian forest, long avoided by Hawaiians, who
feared its strange inhabitants, and by white men, who had no
immediate use for it, finally began to recede, and as the
forest went, the quality and dependability of water went too.
The industry saw the threat, and acted.*

PERHAPS AS recently as the time of Christ, Kauai was
covered with a great native forest. Giant koa and ohia
lehua cast shade for ie-ie and fragile ferns. Hawaiian
loulu palms grew in dense thickets, vying for their places in the
sun on gently rising slopes. The ground cover was tropical,
rich, and various.

How long ago this forest flourished, and when it died, is open
to conjecture, but no human came in time to see it. When the
first Polynesians arrived from Tahiti in their long, double-hulled
canoes, tall reeds had flaunted their brown tassels for centuries
in the Koloa swamp, where the forest once stood. Breezes blowing off the nearby Hoary Head mountains rippled the dark
waters where duck, heron, and mudhen lived undisturbed,
swimming over or wading among the logs of the old forest,
which were to be discovered by white men centuries later.

The forest had retreated to higher ground and stood undisturbed and unknown, except perhaps by the Menehune, Mu,
and Akua. The Menehune, according to Hawaiian legend, were
tiny forest people, very industrious, who worked only at night
and abandoned any project that was not completed by dawn.
They had defeated and driven off most of the Mu people, their
neighbors, in ancient times long before the first Polynesians.
Hawaiians did not fear the Menehune, who were good natured
and whose supernatural power was limited, but they feared the
Akua, who were giant, malevolent, and whose cruel and de-
formed visages were reproduced on Hawaiian masks. Fear of the
Akua kept Hawaiians out of their country. Fear of them, and of
other things in the forest: stones inexplicably warm in the
night, whisperings, sudden violent rainstorms, spirits walking
tall and white in the treetops.

Few Hawaiians ventured into the deep forests—only the bird
collectors, gathering feathers for the great capes of the Alii, and
woodsmen searching for koa canoe logs. These men moved
through the forest without appreciably altering it. The woodsmen took few trees and they left little trace of their presence.
Neither did the bird collectors, called *kiamanu*, though they
made their home in the forests for long periods in their efforts to
supply the bright red, yellow, green, and black feathers demanded by flamboyant kings. Once the needed feathers were
plucked, the birds were set free.

The native Hawaiians confined their trails generally to ridge
tops, from fear of the deep forest below, and there they had
little effect on the woods. The only Hawaiian tools for cutting
canoe logs were stone blades and fire, and the difficulty of the
work prevented cutting more trees than necessary.

Hawaiians began to see more of the wooded mountains late
in the eighteenth century, when the chiefs learned from white
traders of the wealth to be had from selling sandalwood to

China. The fragrant wood had been discovered in 1791 on Kauai by Captain Kendrick. By 1886, when sandalwood logging ceased, the fragrant tree was almost exterminated.

Kamehameha the First's successful military campaigns to conquer all the Hawaiian Islands were undoubtedly financed substantially by the sale of sandalwood in Canton, which enriched the King and chiefs of Hawaii by an estimated three to four million dollars in money and goods. Little of this wealth filtered down to the common people, who sometimes were away in the mountains for several weeks cutting the valuable wood. It sold for from $8.00 to $10.00 a picul (a weight of about 133 pounds), the amount one man could supposedly carry on his back from the forest.

The King's sudden wealth made him easy prey for eager traders, and large drafts on the King's meager cash account compelled him to demand even greater labor from the natives, who were forced to work months in the forest without compensation. When sandalwood became scarce, the King placed a tabu on the wood, reserving it for himself. Large trees that a man could not reach around could not be cut, and the trampling of seedlings was punished by a fine.

The oppression of the chiefs in their drive for personal wealth and service to the King became tyrannical as it became more difficult to find and harvest merchantable logs. The people suffered cruelly, many dying of exposure in the wet mountains. Neglect of taro patches and crops almost precipitated a famine. An annual tax of one picul of sandalwood was levied upon the commoner, who was forced under penalty of fine to bring out even the remaining small crooked sticks, which were fit only for incense in Chinese joss houses. Almost all the larger and more accessible trees had been cut when the sandalwood trade finally ended, and the King was actually in debt, despite the wealth harvested from the Hawaiian forests.

Except for the sandalwood destruction, the white man's coming did not at first greatly change the rain forest. For a time, there was even less forest use. The grotesque temple idols carved from tough ohia were now a forbidden pagan symbol. Spears were no longer needed. The largest, longest, and most magnificent specimens of koa had flourished in the valleys and narrow gulches where they grew high to reach the sun. These had been cut for outrigger canoes and dragged from the forest by ancient routes. But now redwood logs were drifting ashore onto Mahaulepu beach. The chiefs' craftsmen chipped out the California logs into the largest war canoes in Hawaiian waters and soon found the much smaller native koa quite unsatisfactory.

The advent of the sugar industry and the introduction of a money economy also helped to protect the forest. Hawaiians bought cotton instead of making tapa from the stripped and pounded bark of the mamaki and hau trees. Rather than hike into the plentiful forests of ohia and hew timber posts and rafters for their grass huts, collecting armloads of pili grass for thatching and hardwood for poi boards and calabashes, they traded plantation credit coupons at the company store for lumber from Oregon.

Damage to the forest by native Hawaiians had been negligible, however, and any accidental protection the white man gave the forest during his early days in Hawaii was offset by what he did later. After the arrival of cattle and goats on Captain Vancouver's vessels, in 1793, the destruction of Hawaii's forests was inevitable. It was accelerated by the fateful combination of royal tabus on hunting the animals and the absence of hard winters to check their reproduction. There were no predators and there was a limitless food supply. Increasing numbers of pigs added to the forest devastation, and foothills and mountain slopes throughout the kingdom were quickly denuded by feral animals moving higher and higher up the green hillsides. Enormous areas became wastelands as a result of uncontrolled depredation.

As the Hawaiian people slowly died from venereal diseases, measles, smallpox, influenza, and other Old World curses brought in by traders and sailors, so the virgin forest was killed, in many areas to the last tree. Construction of a road or even a trail was invariably followed by death of native trees and ground cover. Few, if any, residents at that time had knowledge of the tropical rain forest and its quick dieback when it is imposed upon, even to the slightest degree. Only a thin layer of humus soil covered the fanlike reach of the ohia lehua root system. The very shallow roots were shaded by delicate ferns and shrubs of the rain-forest ground cover. The luxuriant ie-ie vines hanging from forest trees, the ti and banana plants, and many of the ferns and native sedges could not survive Vancouver's cattle.

By 1815, the wild cattle were recognized as a menace to the forest and their hunting was no longer forbidden, but they continued to multiply rapidly.

Early ranchers on Kauai began to graze the wild cattle commercially as the growing population demanded meat. The native forest was pushed back by the cattle to the edges of Alakai Swamp and the steep pali of Waialeale, and the forest shrank to a tenth of its original size.

Sound range-management practices were unknown or ignored by ranchers, who pushed their cattle continuously onward into the forest as feed was consumed, many times deliberately setting fire to the trees and ground cover to open the way for new feed grasses. Steep palis, shunned altogether by cattle, were laid bare by goats. Wild pigs tore up tree ferns to eat the starchy core.

Grazing lands no longer existed in the lowlands. Where sugar was not growing, earlier farmers had already stripped the land and erosion was far advanced. Huge red scars of exposed earth snaked up the steep ridges, and frequent rain squalls began to soil the blue ocean red where silted throats of mountain streams emptied into the sea. Whaling men in their turn abused the Hawaiian forests. The warm waters of the Pacific and the trade winds of Hawaii made the islands a haven from 1819 to 1871 for the hundreds of Yankee ships searching for whale oil. At times thirty ships waited offshore from tiny Koloa landing. In 1853, 535 whaling vessels visited the Hawaiian Islands, and Koloa on Kauai along with Lahaina, on Maui, became a favored port for semiannual refitting, repairing, and provisioning. Oil and bone were transferred to homeward-bound merchant ships.

Olona fiber, which grew deep inside the wet forest, became prized by the sailors for harpoon lines. Native timbers were used for minor ship repairs, and the kukui forest in the Hoary Head range of Koloa was stripped to provide fuel for the rendering pots.

Later, San Francisco and Monterey on the California coast began gradually to take over the business. The whaling era in Hawaii was brought to a sudden end when a major part of the whaling fleet was destroyed by an early winter in the Arctic ice.

Discovery of gold in California midway in the nineteenth century spurred the sugar industry to expand rapidly to supply the new western market, which was much closer to Hawaii than to southern and Caribbean growers. The early planters were not concerned with preserving the integrity of the native forests, and thousands of acres of virgin jungle were burned to prepare the land for cultivation. Beyond the cane fields, work crews felled trees to supply fuel for the steam-engine boilers of the grinding mills. Then more firewood was cut to boil the raw sugar juice. Some plantations, with an unbelievable lack of foresight, cut into the watersheds that fed their expensive ditch systems.

It was only with the advent of coal and oil-fired boilers, supplemented by dry cane waste, that cutting native timber for fuel began to cease.

Severe insect damage accompanied grazing damage, and portions of native forests were badly hurt by insects which gained a foothold on nearby denuded areas. Insects almost completely defoliated the ohia lehua growing in high, wet valleys. Koa was periodically defoliated by upwards of a dozen insect enemies, which at times have threatened its extinction. The sugar industry's first collaborative program with government agencies began with broad programs to eradicate insects by introducing parasites.

Great forest fires swept woodlands with appalling regularity. Hawaiians started fires to clear small parcels, and trade winds would sweep the flames up pandanus-covered slopes. Probably the most destructive fire in all Hawaii swept the plateau above Mana on Kauai toward the end of the nineteenth century. Valdemar Knudsen, returning in an open boat from the nearby island of Niihau, saw a rising cloud of smoke and quickly made for Kauai, but by the time he and his men arrived in the uplands, the entire forest was aflame. It was impossible to stop the fire, and it burned for weeks, scorching the ridge of distant Milolii Valley on Napali, before a torrential rainstorm drowned the flames. More than 10,000 acres of native forest, already injured by wild cattle and ruinous overgrazing practices, was destroyed in the blaze.

What the cattle overlooked and fire failed to engulf, man removed in a consuming desire to get rich on the newly available lands of Hawaii, which were obtainable for little investment beyond the cost of land clearing.

Small sugar growers proliferated rapidly and as quickly failed; their lack of agricultural knowledge and insufficient operating capital doomed their enterprises, leaving the cleared forest lands temporarily abandoned to rank weeds and rapidly eroding gullies. Others planted coffee, mulberry, cotton, and various commercial crops that also failed. There was such an abundance of land that few businessmen questioned the feasibility of their projected planting. If they had, thousands of acres of fertile land would have been saved. A planters' Gold Rush swept the Islands, to be eventually stopped by concerted efforts of the very sugar monopoly repeatedly criticized for selfish exploitation of Hawaii's land.

The destruction of the forest began to concern the sugar planters, who were among the first to realize that remedial action was needed. They moved quickly to recreate the forests that had held water for the irrigation of their vast sugar fields, before increasing soil erosion and polluted water sources endangered the recharging ability of underground water tables. In 1876, by request of the sugar growers, the King proclaimed a law for "the protection and preservation of woods and forests" and actually set aside an area of the upper lands of Hamakua and Kohala on the Island of Hawaii as a forest preserve—but little was done to enforce the early law.

Shortly before the Kingdom was overthrown by annexationists, Queen Liliuokalani signed into law legislation that exempted from taxes private lands exclusively used to protect watersheds. Approved in 1892, the unique law stated that "The preservation of forests is a matter of great public interest in consequence of their influence upon the water supply of the Kingdom," and provided that "where land is fenced to protect the forest, springs or streams, and all livestock is excluded and no other use is made of the land, the owner will be exempt from taxes."

Actual forest reserves were not established by the Queen, and the large sugar plantation owners became more and more frightened by the continued destruction of the forest lands by unrestrained ranching operations.

Sanford Dole, in one of his first acts as new President of the Provisional Government of Hawaii, created a Bureau of Forestry and Agriculture in 1892, and reforestation work began on the bare, denuded hills back of Honolulu and the slopes of Punchbowl Crater.

With communication with Washington a difficult procedure and political forces of the deposed Queen still at work, a Constitutional Convention met in May 1894 and drafted a constitution for a Republic, which was proclaimed on July 4th, with Dole as its first president. The new Republic had many problems to meet and had little opportunity to develop a sound program for reforestation, although government and businessmen both realized the need and importance of a fully implemented forestry program. Many years were still to pass before the first forest reserve was actually established.

Hawaii was warned again in an 1895 report from the Minister of the Interior, who expressed his concern that:

The destruction of forests in this country is a serious matter. Large areas of land have within recent years become deforested, and the effect on the climate in those regions is shown by the decreased rainfall. Ninety-nine percent of this destruction has and is being caused by cattle. It is most unfortunate that so large an amount of the public domain has been leased for grazing purposes, nearly all the forest lands are now under lease to cattle raisers, and unless something is soon done to preserve the limited amount of remaining forests they will, in a short time, be all destroyed.

Four years later, the Bureau of Forestry and Agriculture presented to the Republic the first detailed report on forest islands in 1899. In describing Kauai's Kalaheo forests he said:

Hundreds of acres of this forest land have been destroyed by cattle; hundreds of trees are dead and dying, and only a small portion of the forest close to the mountain ridge remains intact. Ninety per cent of the cattle I saw are in an advanced stage of tuberculosis—and some of

the animals were mere walking skeletons too weak to brush off the horn flies. None of the cattle were fit for human food. On the lowlands near the sea, the cattle were in fair condition. If the McBryde Sugar Company do not take steps to fence off this forest land at once and [provide for] removal of worthless cattle, our government should take advantage of our forest laws and cancel the lease.

In the same report, Herberts writes of the Lihue Plantation's leased lands at Wailua, Kauai:

On this land is an immense forest in excellent condition, fenced off from river to river, and any domestic animals found within the enclosure are shot. This plantation has also hundreds of acres of young and thrifty forest trees. . . . The result is that the Lihue Plantation has water to give away, while other parts of the island are short. It is an established fact that the destruction of forests in any country tends to diminish the supply of water. Let any one doubting this fact visit the Lihue Plantation and be convinced.

Island ranchers strongly objected when the sugar planters offered to construct, at their own expense, miles of fences to close off the remaining forests to grazing. The ranchers claimed that the fences would cut off their cattle from feed and water during dry periods in the lowlands, though they admitted that if grazing continued in the forest, it would simply be a question of time before the remaining forest was destroyed and the existing water sources disappeared permanently. Even the ranchers were threatened with ruin if the destructive grazing practices were continued.

Early in the twentieth century, Harold Lyons was employed by the sugar industry to bring order to land management before the sugar industry was ruined. He imported a handful of mainland foresters to plan a reforestation program and to investigate the nature of Hawaiian forests. The Hawaiian Sugar Planters Association took the lead in 1902, when they organized a special committee to consult with Sanford Dole, then first Governor of the Territory of Hawaii. Dole accepted their proposals and appointed men named by the sugar industry to designate forest reservation boundaries on private and public lands. The 1903 legislature, following the governor's recommendations, passed the first Territorial law providing for the establishment of forest reservations.

With the objective of devising ways and means to halt the forest destruction, and to determine forest reserve boundaries, government-appointed foresters, recruited and paid by the Sugar Planters Association, visited the ravaged forests and called meetings of planters and ranchers.

The voice of sugar became dominant not only in Hawaii's economy and politics, but also in a plea for conservation of the land.

But there was one tree specially dedicated to Kauai, and it made both life and agriculture on the island possible. Wherever the powerful northeast trades whipped sea and salt air inland, killing everything that grew, men had planted the strange, silky, gray-green casuarina tree, known sometimes as the ironwood. Groves of this curious tree, covered with ten-inch needles and seed cones that resembled round buttons, stood along the shore and protected the island. The foliage of the casuarina was not copious and to the stranger each tree looked so frail that it seemed about to die, but it possessed incredible powers of recuperation, and what it thrived on most was a harsh, salty trade wind that whipped its fragile needles into a frenzy and tore at its cherry-bark trunk; for then the casuarina dug in and saved the island. The sea winds howled through its branches; its frail needles caught the salt; the force of the storm was broken and all who lived in the shadow of the casuarina tree lived securely.

—JAMES MICHENER, *Hawaii*

5. Pandora's Box

Moving to save the Kauaian forests, with the best of intentions, the industry's foresters made a bad mistake.

NAPALI-KONA FOREST was proclaimed a forest reserve in 1907. Puukapele followed in 1917. The Kauai Planters Association, financed by the Island's sugar industry, hired the first Kauai forester, Albert Duval, in 1928. Three quarters of his salary was paid by the planters. Fences were raised around the forest reserves as rapidly as the boundaries were proclaimed by the Governor. Duval began a program to clear the forests of wild cattle and goats. In 1926 alone 25,178 animals, 6,000 of them goats, had been killed in the Territory. Duval, assisted by local hunters, soon was killing an average of 100 goats a month on Kauai alone. The total extermination program advocated by Territorial Forester C. S. Judd might have succeeded had not Eric Knudsen and others urged that some cattle and goats be left to keep the trails open.

Reduction of forest cover had resulted in adverse modification of climatic conditions, and the influence of the forest upon both the amount and the distribution of rainfall became a matter of common knowledge in Hawaii. The point was reached at which the industry had to restore the balance. Some plantations, on fee-simple land, began planting forests as part of individual reforestation programs. Hans Isenberg, of Lihue Plantation, replanted several hundred acres near Lihue town that had previously been cut over for fuel. Another 10,000 acres of uncut forest above the plantation's extensive ditch system was sealed off with miles of cattle-proof fence and closed to the public. The Kalepa Hills, which had been stripped of sandalwood by the chiefs and of kukui firewood for the Hanamaulu Mill, were replanted in ironwood.

But encroachment continued. In many areas, plantation managers continued to clear new land, often overruling limits prescribed by guidelines of their own industry. Many homesteaders cleared the land, marketed the timber, and then turned over their acreage to the plantation, finding it more profitable to sell homestead lands and work for the plantations than to farm the land themselves. Ranchers did not share the concern of the planters, and continued to show resistance to any reforestation program.

In 1907 the first large-scale attempt to process Hawaiian timber for export began when a shipment of more than 13,000 ohia lehua railroad ties were sent to California from Hawaii Island. The Santa Fe Railroad contracted for 90 million board feet of island hardwood. Small amounts of koa were also exported to the mainland as "Hawaiian mahogany."

The greatest damage to the native forests during this period

was not done by loggers or by ranchers, but by foresters in their attempts to rebuild the watersheds. The early foresters, with inadequate academic training and insufficient time for experimental work, had difficulty replanting native trees and concluded that it could not be done. In areas where goats and cattle were controlled, the natural reseeding was abundant and new growth of koa, ohia, and even sandalwood flourished, but it was easy to replant with exotic species and foresters decided to do so.

Thousands of trees were planted in a blind haste to replant the land. Recklessly, without regard to the consequences to Hawaii's shrinking native forests, the sugar-financed government program opened what botanist Otto Degener has called a "Pandora's Box of biological evils," in order to save the watersheds. Seeds of alien plants were distributed to all islands in great quantities to be planted by plantation workers and volunteers, without plan or program.

Botanists retained by the sugar industry roamed the globe, gathering seeds and cuttings for grasses and trees from dozens of countries in the Caribbean and Pacific. Japan, Australia, and New Zealand alone contributed countless varieties of trees and shrubs, including Japanese cedar and giant chestnut, teak, rubber, cacao, sisal, black wattle, various species of eucalyptus, acacia, albizia, Mexican ash, silk oak, orange, and lemon guava.

The botanists ignored the fact that Hawaii's indigenous plants were in a very delicate state of health, and that the slightest interference from man or his hoofed animals so disturbed their ecological balance that rapid deterioration and death inevitably followed. Large numbers of exotic shrubs, weeds, grasses, and trees introduced into the Islands found local conditions well suited to their reproduction. They spread rapidly, assuming forms and agressiveness not revealed in their native habitats, immediately occupying areas vacated by native plants, crowding out native seedlings and young plants. As a consequence, the reforestation program initiated to save the watersheds served to smother the native forest. In many areas the native forest continued to die back, and its place was taken by weeds and thorny shrubs.

Hawaiian flora would have retained a remarkable integrity if plant introduction had not occurred. Yet saving the watershed undoubtedly saved the sugar industry from ruin. The experiments with eucalyptus, paperbark, firebush, monkeypod, ironwood, black wattle, Monterey cypress, and silk oak were successful.

Probably the first trees planted in the Kauai mountains were planted by Ranger Albert MacDonald in 1928. They were 100 seedlings of Kauai's indigenous acacia, kauaiensis, and the 324 acacia koa around the Kanalohuluhulu meadow in Kokee. In the same year, Albert Duval traveled by horseback to the edge of Alakai Swamp along Waialae Stream and planted ten California redwood and fifteen firebush seedlings.

Numerous varieties of trees continued to be introduced throughout the islands without any over-all plan. In 1929, the Army Air Corps, as a community service, helped the foresters sow seed in denuded areas of Puukapele, Kokee, and Napali From a Fokker C-2 monoplane, fifty-eight pounds of New Zealand karaka seed, which turned out to be poisonous, were scattered on higher slopes of Alakai from 2,000 feet above the swamp. A total of 1,689 pounds of seed was sown from the air at random over a widespread area. Most of these were Pride of India seeds, but included were Chinese fan palm, ironwood, Java plum, eucalyptus robusta, and African tulip. Also sown were seeds of two natives, kukui and loulu palm.

The game warden at Kokee planted Oregon ash, dogwood, elderberry and huckleberry, and liberated twenty-four young guinea fowl. The mongrel forest of Kokee continued to grow.

Wild cattle, goats, and pigs, with no natural enemies, continued to threaten the planting program. Duval estimated that 20 per cent of new tree losses were to wild pig rooting, and 10 per cent from the Uluhe fern, which smothered young seedlings.

On his first inspection trip to Kalalau Valley after the old Hawaiian Napali trail was cleared by the county in early 1933, Duval reported to Chief Forester Judd on the continued overgrazing by cattle, which had practically exterminated ferns and ti on the ridges. He wrote, "Cattle foraging on the steep slopes during wet weather have cut trails into the soft earth creating channels whereby soil is being washed into the ocean." On the same trip, he noted many wild goats, "as many as 40 in a single herd." Wild cattle and goats still roamed the forests in great numbers, contributing to continued erosion and to destruction of plants along Napali.

Probably the most destructive exotic plant introduction occurred about 1920, when a young plantation manager, Dave Larsen, carried to Kokee several cuttings of Himalayan blackberries, planting them in the backyard of his mountain cabin on Noe stream. Neighbor Charlie Rice apprehensively watched the blackberry spread into the forest, and he notified Territorial Forester Judd of the potential danger to Kokee. Although the cabin owners pulled the brambles from their own yards, the territory neglected to take similar measures on forest lands. It was not until several years later that Territorial Ranger MacDonald saw blackberry sprouts growing along the Waineke trail and began pulling up every shoot in sight. He traced the berry to Larsen's then-abandoned cabin, and with the help of a CCC crew, swiftly dug up the original blackberry patch, now grown into a wild tangle of thorns. They cut out the roots and sifted the soil. But within a year, new sprouts appeared in the woods. The blackberries had escaped. Birds soon spread them throughout Kokee, where their vines gradually smothered the life from ferns and ground cover.

During World War II, all forestry programs stopped. The Army took over the mountains of Kauai, and during four war years the blackberry grew unrestricted. MacDonald returned after the war and was shocked at what he found. "I was sick when I saw the backberries everywhere," he said. "They were too far gone to stop them."

Other foreign exotics had escaped and spread through the tropical forest. The bright nasturtiums were first planted by Ebba Faye in the yard of her mountain house at Halemanu. Early construction workers planted the hanging pink lilikoi around their bunk dormitories for food while digging the Kekaha irrigation tunnels in 1923. Calla lilies were first seen about the same time. Montbretia, the small bright red lily, was well-established by 1905. The purple flowered "Isenberg bush" was brought to Kauai from the foothills of the Himalayas by Dora

Isenberg and carefully tended in her garden. The attractive tibouchina plant soon escaped from her Lihue home and spread into the foothills of Kilohana crater. In about 1909 Mrs. Abner Wilcox brought from Honolulu a small multiblossomed lantana plant potted in a red bowl. She enjoyed the tiny orange and pink blossoms for many years until the plant grew too large for the porch. Her gardener threw it out on the trash pile, from where it eventually spread to all parts of the island. The bush grew into impenetrable thickets and thrived on the dry ridges and flats laid bare by goats and cattle. Guava, another exotic, grew into impenetrable thickets, gradually choking out competitive plant life. Java plum filled gulches from rim to rim and native plants completely disappeared.

The tropical forest beauty was slowly and irretrievably being replaced by a synthetic forest. Human experiments were changing the shape and color of the land. Broad carpets of a giant grass, sugar cane, covered the flatlands between gulches. Many streams never reached the sea in summer months, their full flow intercepted by complex irrigation systems and carried to the thirsty cane fields which consumed many times more water than a city covering the same area would have.

Gray patterns of pineapples covered plateaus in geometric forms, and contour planting began to reshape the land on upper hillsides. Kauai, as first sighted by the Polynesians, was barely recognizable. Efforts to stimulate economic development had succeeded beyond all measure. The government encouraged importation of European labor. Workers came in large numbers from Portugal, Germany, England, Scotland, and Norway. Contract workers left their homes in China and Japan for promises of new wealth in Hawaii. Grants of land to foreigners to encourage permanent settlers changed the tiny Island Kingdom's subsistence economy to a modern money economy, and into a territory of the United States. As the twentieth century began, Hawaii was able to boast of exports totalling $29 million a year.

But Hawaii had become poorer by another measure. Its native forests were virtually destroyed and would never recover. In less than 150 years, man had destroyed a forest and an ecosystem that was 20 to 30 million years in the making.

Koa forest, Kokee

6. Kokee

*Its beauty rediscovered by industry employees and
their families, the Kokee country's secret was out,
and a new movement began.*

FROM THE time Valdemar Knudsen first turned his
herd into the uplands of Kokee, ranchers had grazed
cattle in the high forests there. Later sugar planters came
and marveled at the wonders of Kokee as they supervised the
digging of the extensive irrigation ditches and tunnels which
were to divert water from mountain streams along the upper rim
of Waimea Canyon. They were among the first to enjoy a wilderness experience in the natural beauty of Kokee. These transient
visitors slowly became aware of their responsibility toward the
forest and the need for its care and preservation.

Conservation became the law of the land. Conservation to
save the sugar industry, however, not conservation for recreation
or timber production. Multiple use of any sort was still frowned
upon as potentially harmful to the watershed.

Kauai's forest lands were ringed with cattle-proof fences and
padlocked. Even public picnicking and camping were discouraged. Hunting continued by cowboys and plantation workers, but primarily as a means to supplement their food. Effective
game management did not exist. Tourism had not been thought
of, nor was it ever considered that any economic activity could
replace sugar.

But recreation began in the forests of Kokee, in spite of the
fences. The wagon trail along the rim of Waimea Canyon was
gradually improved and soon Kauai's first automobiles clashed
gears on the steep grades out of Kekaha. Knudsen's friends discovered the cool, invigorating air of Kokee and built small
cabins of their own in the forest. Lumber was hauled up the
winding road, and an exclusive mountain community quickly
developed on Knudsen-leased land at Halemanu.

Governor Charles J. McCarthy made his first visit to the
Kokee mountains on vacation after World War I. He agreed
that more land should be opened up for cabins, and 415 acres
were withdrawn from the Kekaha ranch lease. By proclamation
of the Governor, the land was transferred to the County of
Kauai, which leased the cabin sites. Surveys of the land were
vague, and in the spirit of the time, the boundary corner monu-
ment along Waimea Canyon rim was described in the proclamation as "a mound of stones around trunk of leaning koa tree."
It is no wonder that the exact acreage and location of the first
county park on Kauai was not determined for many years.

The Governor of Hawaii, following a visit to Kokee in 1929,
expressed a desire to increase the area of protected forest reserve and to include the road area along the rim of Waimea
Canyon, "the idea being to preserve the koa trees along this
road for the scenic effect."

Forester Judd personally inspected the area on the ground on
a three-day survey trip and came to the conclusion that an area
of almost 9,000 acres could be added to the Puukapele Forest

Reserve without impairing ranching operations, which were marginal at best. Most of the land, especially along the seacoast, was relatively inaccessible country, much of it covered with scrub forest growth and just beginning to recover from the damaging 1890 range fire.

Some meadows and pockets of good grazing existed among the recovering groves of koa trees at the head of small gulches along Waimea Canyon, and it was from these sections that Forester Judd especially wanted all stock excluded "so as to give the young tree growth a chance to mature." In his report, Judd pointed out that "the constant nibbling by cattle and horses of young koa seedlings and root sprouts and the smashing of young koa trees by cattle . . . simply holds back the growth development of the trees. So long as grazing is permitted . . . proper tree growth and a satisfactory undercover of shrubs and other vegetation will not be obtained . . . The practice of allowing grazing on areas where it is desired to have and maintain native forest growth has become archaic."

However, the continuing requirements of the ranchers, who grazed their cattle with little restraint and without proper range management practices, were not to be ignored. C. T. Bailey, Commissioner of Public Lands, was obviously not convinced of the necessity of expanding forest reserves in 1929 to accelerate recovery of the native forest. He informed Forester Judd that his proposal "seems inadvisable on account of the grazing value of this land . . . with the resultant loss of rental to the Territory and the economic loss in curtailing the production of cattle." Instead of Judd's 9,000 acres, Bailey recommended the forest expansion be limited to approximately 750 acres, almost all along the Waimea Canyon Rim Road. The compromise left more than 8,000 acres of slowly recovering forest land exposed to continued depredation by cattle.

In August 1930, 755 acres were added to the Puukapele Forest Reserve, including the small groves of koa and ohia lehua, and growths of new sandalwood and native hibiscus. Within a few years, these 755 acres, insufficient as they might be, were proclaimed the Waimea Canyon Territorial Park.

In 1941, Joseph F. Kunesh, director of the short-lived Territorial Planning Board, stated that:

Although the Territory owns over one and a half million acres in 9,600 parcels well distributed on all the islands and controls over a million acres of public and private forest reserve lands, there are in Hawaii today practically no Territorial parks, no Territorial parkways, no Territorial monuments, or no Territorial memorials.

Ten years later, following the end of World War II, the words were almost as true as when first written. The planters' policy of closed forest reserves not only had prevented the establishment of a timber industry, but also had stopped the formation of a modern Territorial park system.

The National Park Service observed in a report for the Terri-

tory that "It is doubtful if a completely successful park and recreation program can be achieved in the Territory without a higher degree of participation by private citizens, organizations, and most especially the large land holders, than seems to have been provided heretofore . . . a favorable 'climate' is the first prerequisite for programs of this order."

Growing public clamor for mountain parks soon made itself heard, however, and the Territorial government, while still sympathetic to the contrary wishes of the sugar industry, could hardly ignore the growing Hawaiian middle class who desired outdoor recreation and pointed out the famed California system of state parks as an example for Hawaii to follow.

Hawaiian residents began traveling more widely on the mainland, and their favorable experiences in popular state parks strongly influenced local politicians. Territorial Representative Manuel Aguiar of Kauai early in 1947 asked the Board of Agriculture and Forestry, who had jurisdiction over Territorial lands, to make Kokee and Napali a state park. Colin G. Lennox, president of the Board, prepared an administration bill to establish a Kokee Territorial Park on forest reserve lands. Introduced in 1947, the bill never left committee in the Republican, planter-dominated legislature.

Public disappointment over these events and growing awareness of the need for care and protection of the forest lands caused many community organizations to discuss alternate ways and means of opening up the mountain lands of Kauai for public use. Possibly the first citizen plea for a national park on Kauai resulted from this frustrated political agitation for a Territorial park in Kokee. The Hanapepe Civic Association wrote Colin Lennox after the 1947 legislature adjourned without bringing about a Kokee Park, saying, "Frankly, the National Park Service should have established several areas on the island of Kauai as national parks, especially that of the Kokee and Napali coast." They added further that "This Association will back any effort that you make or endorse in regard to national parks on the island of Kauai." The seed for a national park was planted early by the people of Kauai.

Two years later, Act 185 of the 1949 legislature called for withdrawal of 4,451 acres from the Napali-Kona Forest Reserve and set aside the lands as a Territorial Park. Cheers by park supporters were muted somewhat by the discovery that no funds were appropriated for the infant park. Also, the boundaries were not selected on the basis of recreation or scenic potential, but rather to connect existing survey points in order to make a field survey unnecessary. Three years passed before Governor Oren E. Long on May 15, 1952, officially proclaimed the existence of the Kokee Territorial Park and construction began on the first true public facilities: a natural history museum, to be staffed by volunteers; a grocery store; and four rental cabins, all constructed mostly from surplus army camp materials. Kokee had finally become a public park.

Alakai Swamp

7. New Foresters

The old foresters had made Pandora's mistake;
they were followed by men who knew better, and the
forest had a new chance.

ON THE eve of the Japanese attack on Pearl Harbor, a single-use philosophy of forest management still prevailed in the Territorial Department of Agriculture and Forestry. Regional parks were practically non-existent. Kokee was a weekend playground for the upper class. The public was rarely seen in the mountains of Kauai before World War II, except as guests of private cabin owners, and the only public facility was the small picnic pavilion constructed by the County at Puukapele.

For many years, ranchers continued to encroach upon the forest reserve boundaries—even when they were altered in their favor. In order that ranch land would qualify as tax-free forest reserve, miles of fence were strung across gulches and ridges by cowboys, who used wire and ohia posts supplied by the Territory, only to have trespassers cut the smooth wire and allow cattle to enter the reserve. In his monthly reports, Kauai forester Duval made repeated references to violations by neighboring ranchers when he found branded cattle and horses grazing within the forest reserve, in addition to remnants of the vast herds of wild longhorns, goats, and pigs. Cattle and horses were often seen grazing on forest lands in Waialae Valley and Kaholuamanu, adjacent to Alakai Swamp. Kekaha Ranch cowboys helped Duval drive out thirty horses on one inspection trip. Wild cattle found within the boundary were always shot.

A progressive island-born forester, Eric Reppun, was appointed new president of the Board of Agriculture and Forestry by the first part-Hawaiian governor, Samuel Wilder King, to take on the task of changing completely the philosophy of a department held tightly in the grip of the sugar planters for 40 years. The forests had been locked up and unused—except as the large land owners wanted them available for expansion of pasture or cane. The forest reserve laws were written to allow assignment of privately owned land to forest reserves—where the land would be free from taxes—yet permitted withdrawal of the land at any time on ten days' notice. Not until 1957 were these liberal surrender agreements changed to halt the establishment of temporary forest reserves to avoid land taxes while the land was held for future use.

The planters and large landowners lost much of their control over the land with passage of new land laws in 1957. Reppun proceeded to eliminate industry influence over the Division of Forestry and to restore the prestige of the Territorial Forester and the Board of Agriculture and Forestry. The board members unwittingly had become titular figures in Honolulu who simply approved actions the island associate forester had often already performed. The old Board of Agriculture and Forestry seldom met and internal communication had suffered, with the result that the associate forester usually ran his own island and developed policies as he saw fit, without guidelines based on long-term best interests of the people of the Territory.

The island foresters were really only custodians—and too often only self-made naturalists. Their old habits were not easily broken. The established foresters were the same men who

years before had been selected by the Hawaiian Sugar Planters Association, hired by the Territory and paid by the Planters Association. Their wages were now paid by the Territory, but their loyalties were to the planters, and the old timers somewhat resented the new personnel and the new programs. To them, the interests of the sugar industry were identical with the interests of the Territory. They resisted the new young men in Honolulu who wanted wider use of the forest—a complete departure from the planters' idea. Reppun was the first appointed forester not a part of the Establishment, and he was severely criticized by the planters' representatives for breaking with traditional patterns of forest management that had served industry so well over the years.

Reppun died before he was able to complete the long-needed overhaul of the forestry division. The Territorial Governor picked Wayne Collins to carry on Reppun's program. Collins, the last president of the Board of Agriculture and Forestry, resigned his position as a popular Honolulu television news director and prepared to implement the new concepts of forest use. For his deputy, Collins appointed Hawaii Island forester Bill Bryan, who traveled tirelessly to every island and convinced the old-timers of the new program's rightness. Islanders still speak of Bryan as the "old tough man" who, in six months, was able to get a commercial timber planting program under way for the "young tough man," as the independent and somewhat uncompromising Collins was called. Together they accomplished the job of transforming Hawaii's forest policy.

For the first time since the days of the CCC, improvements were made on recreation trails. Collins ordered the removal of miles of forest reserve fences, opening the reserves for public recreation and park use. He laid the groundwork for a new public appreciation of forest lands.

The government of Hawaii, through Collins, was responding to the wishes of a larger number of people as the fiftieth state savored its first taste of statehood.

Terns, Kalalau Beach

8. *Kalalau and the Road*

*The most beautiful valley of the Napali coast, undisturbed
until the twentieth century, was threatened suddenly and
in turn by cattle, lantana, wild cats, and politicians.*

IN THE ancient days, Hawaiians living in the hanging valleys of Napali on the north coast of Kauai celebrated important events with a great feast and native fireworks. A favorite place for the rare events was remote Nualolo Kai, a shallow valley with a beach at its mouth and a half-moon reef arching out into the sea. At the evening's climax when all had finished their feasting and drunk their brew of okolehao, young children climbed to the top of the high vertical cliffs guarding Nualolo. Here were piles of hau and hollow papala branches, gathered earlier from the mountains and cut into lengths of ten and twenty feet. Fires were lighted and as the dry, light sticks blazed, they were pushed from the pali into space, and the evening winds carried them far out to sea. Then darker night

closed in, and the villagers and chiefs slept where they had gathered on the beach.

Hawaiian village fires were burning in adjacent Nualolo Aina Valley at least 700 years ago, as evidenced by carbon dates determined by Bishop Museum archeologists. Thriving communities flourished in the narrow valleys. The Napali taro plant, famous throughout the kingdom for its keeping qualities, was cultivated in the deep black earth. Stone-walled terraces and diversion ditches feeding water to the taro patches completely covered the valley floor. House platforms were built high on the talus slopes or wedged between terrace dikes so they would not infringe on the valuable taro land.

This traditional way of life continued into very recent times, but began to change as Hawaiians became more and more aware of the white man's offer of what might be a better life, and as the fertility of the land and the need for its produce changed with the times. Rancher Selwyn Robinson, who had become the largest individual landowner on Kauai, forsaw a voluntary Hawaiian emigration, and in return for deeds to their kuleanas, provided the necessary cash for Hawaiians to buy Chinese rice, clothes from the merchants, white man's lumber, and to send their children to missionary schools. Robinson allowed the Hawaiians to continue to live on the kuleanas and harvest the taro, but they soon yearned for the new amenities away from the valley and, by 1914, the valley of Kalalau and its rich taro lands were abandoned. Robinson claimed fee simple ownership or majority interest in 156 acres of unlocated kuleanas—the only private land in Kalalau Valley.

Robinson obtained a long-term lease on the remaining government lands, and shipped in cattle to fatten on the rich grasses of Kalalau. As the grass was consumed, thickets of lantana and guava grew across the valley and into the abandoned taro terraces. The cattle denuded much of their grazing land, eating seedlings of native trees and every blade of sprouting grass. In places only the lantana and guava remained—apparently distasteful even to the hungry animals. The proliferating seeds spread out across the valley, sticking to the hides of foraging cattle or carried by tropic birds to the most remote ravines. Hoofs broke down the carefully constructed terraces and dikes, destroying native house platforms and heiau temples. Village sites disappeared in whirling dust fields, and once carefully tended taro terraces disappeared under silt and weeds.

Today the destruction continues. Kalalau is a virtual no man's land—neither forest reserve nor state park, rather a combination ranch and campground with no one assuming responsibility for its care or maintenance. Hunters, arriving by boat and helicopter, roam the valley, mixing among family hiking groups and picnickers, shooting goats on the fluted cliffs, sometimes recovering the animals, but more often than not leaving them to rot. Campers themselves show little inclination to clean up when their surroundings are so misused. Wild cats roam free, killing rare birds and robbing nests. The songs of Hawaiian birds—once filling the air with their haunting calls—have begun to disappear along with the native trees and endemic plants in which they built their nests.

Only Kalalau's size and its relative inaccessibility have kept it the most beautiful valley in the Pacific. So far the abuse has been on a scale that nature can handle. The four-thousand-foot cliffs, long waterfalls, and white beaches are still unsurpassed in all Hawaii.

The greatest present threat to Kalalau's beauty is the bulldozer. Many local residents have long dreamed of a scenic highway around the island connecting the dead-end country roads at Kokee and Haena and crossing the spectacular cliffs of Napali, the hanging valley of Hanakoa and Alakai Swamp. The obvious economic impracticality of a road through the mountains, and the ravage of the scenic Napali wilderness by a ruinous cut-and-fill highway, does not concern them. The road would divert into the heart of Kauai's greatest scenery all the obnoxious noise and smell of every truck, car, and motorcycle crossing the island,

using Kokee Park as a handy shortcut, and would result in destruction of the wilderness that the first major territorial park in Hawaii was designed to protect.

In 1949, over the opposition of island hotels and tour companies, Senator Noburo Miyake, the chief proponent of the road, sought funds for it in the senate. He was unsuccessful, and the money was diverted to other more practical Kauai roads.

Hotel operators opposed the road on purely economic grounds, arguing that tourists wouldn't visit long on Kauai—they could see the island in one day and return to Honolulu without staying overnight. Miyake continued to argue for the road, pointing out that many construction jobs would result and that the road would open up land for subdivision and roadside business.

Through the years many people in power on Kauai looked on Kokee-Napali as an area for economic development without considering the far greater values of Kokee Park for public enjoyment of wilderness experience and for protection of the unique natural scenic resources of Napali.

Gross ignorance of park values was revealed in a 1950 territorial legislative resolution calling for a feasibility study of a highway serving northwestern Kauai. The resolution stated:

Whereas other areas of natural beauty such as Nualolo, Milolii, Kalalau and Hanakapiai are relatively inaccessible for lack of good roads, but possess great potential for development, not only for the tourist trade, but also for agriculture, ranching and fishing, this area . . . could be opened for development if adequate roads were built.

The Public Works Feasibility Report released in 1951 should have discouraged anyone interested in the road; it said in conclusion: "that the benefits that could be expected by the construction of any of the above roads would not meet the heavy cost of their construction. The construction of roads . . . would not, therefore, be economically feasible."

The report dismissed the idea of a shore road built along the Napali-Kalalau Trail and beyond to Barking Sands as "too impractical to merit any further consideration."

Joining the opposition with a unanimous Board of Directors' resolution in 1953, the Kauai Chamber of Commerce opposed the projected road as "being prohibitive to maintain" and added:

The Kauai Chamber of Commerce does not feel there is any necessity for having a road completely around the island of Kauai, nor is there an economic need for such a road . . . tour drive companies would probably lose some business by having a round-the-island road.

But the County Board of Supervisors, faced with increasing unemployment on Kauai in 1954, saw the projected road as an excellent make-work project using public funds, and they justified the destructive road, saying:

The route would open an area of 120 square miles for ranching, truck farming, fruit orchards, sugar and pineapple, with substantial portions of the area suitable for cattle ranching.

They argued it would lead to construction of hotels in the Kokee area, and stated further that "forest reserve areas designated as part of the park system may be leased to individuals for commercial development." The military value of such a road was also mentioned, and it was pointed out that "during World War II military authorities had seriously contemplated a similar road to facilitate troop movements."

Lichen, Kalalau Valley

Puu Ki from Kalalau Valley Lookout

Ten thousand dollars was advanced out of the Territorial General Fund for construction of a Kokee-Haena road "by prison labor."

The highway department's survey crew followed the bulldozers in a classic "push and go" clearing operation, uprooting portions of the only native forest on Kauai that remained untouched by fire or cattle. Ohia lehua and ancient koa trees were felled with no public protest by the division of forestry, administrators of the park, or citizen organizations on Kauai.

The forest had no apologist to defend it and died under the onslaught. In eight months the money was gone and the bulldozers were mired. A swath of destruction four miles long ended in the quagmire of Alakai Swamp. Men could do no better against the combined resistance of Kauai's finest forest, 120 inches of yearly rainfall, chilly fogs, and slippery clay soil.

Upon further statements by Public Works that the project "does not appear to be economically feasible because of its high costs," requests for additional money were refused. "Miyake's Folly" went no farther.

The damaged ridge above Kalalau has now eroded and dumped ancient topsoil down the walls of the valley, exposing the saddle between Kalalau and Waimea canyons to possible breakthrough. These and other scars of the abortive roadway are apparent to anyone there, but the lesson is not to those who are in power on Kauai.

Few of Kauai's public officials or its leading citizens appear to appreciate the great spiritual value of Kauai's scenery or to understand that it must be protected. The road will remain a danger as long as Napali is unprotected. Work on the road will be renewed whenever a politician thinks he sees his chance.

Radar dome, Kokee

9. *Antennae*

*The Kokee forest, profoundly altered but still beautiful,
was invaded by the military, and the Kokee foresters
faced one of the greatest threats to their wilderness.*

HIGH-RANKING officers of the Hawaii Air National Guard's air defense command visited Maui Island in 1959 and spoke of job opportunities, economic development, and payrolls in a series of well-planned meetings with service clubs and business leaders throughout Maui. Their job was to soften resistance from conservationists and gain support from the community for their request to construct a radar system high on the 10,000-foot rim of Haleakala Crater in the Maui section of Hawaii National Park. Secretary of the Interior Seaton, speaking for the National Park Service, said "no."

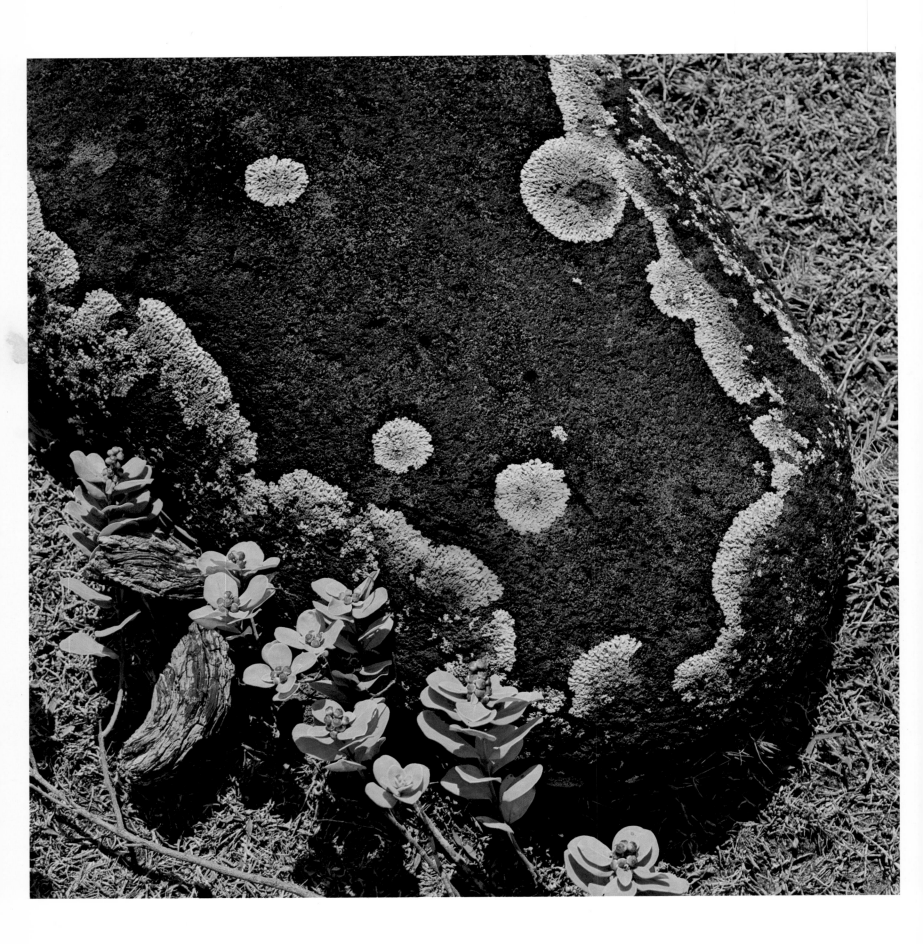

Despite impassioned pleas of its importance to the national defense and its protection of Hawaii from enemy attack, no military radar was constructed on Maui.

Shortly after the Maui incident a similar team of Air National Guard officers appeared on Kauai. The Deputy Commander of the Hawaiian Air Defense spoke to forty civic leaders at a June luncheon in Lihue, asking their support of his efforts to obtain a site for expansion of Hawaii's early warning radar network, which, he said, would also include Oahu and Maui, "to monitor all aircraft entering the Hawaii Air Defense identification zone." He again emphasized the money to be spent and the new job opportunities for Kauai residents. Many Kauai businessmen voiced unqualified support for the installation, without asking the location, although rumor placed it in Kokee State Park. In Honolulu, park supporters objected, but were met with arguments that the installation was important to national defense and with assurances that it was only a temporary measure.

Unknown to supporters and opponents alike, the site had been already selected by the Air Force five months earlier. In official, unpublished correspondence were statements by the Corps of Engineers that "plans called for long-term operation of the station."

Without seriously questioning where the site was or if there would be infringement of park values, the Commissioner of Public Lands granted right of entry for immediate start of the project, and the National Guard began construction by winter of 1959. When the early spring visitors to Kokee arrived, the entrance to Kalalau Lookout, offering the most magnificent panoramic view in all Hawaii, was slashed and desecrated by a monstrous radar dome and array of communications antennae. The continuous whine of electronic equipment pierced the silence of Kokee and destroyed the once-peaceful solitude and grandeur of Kalalau.

Very much later, on September 1, 1965, the State signed a lease agreement with the Air National Guard for the eight-acre radar site at Kalalau—six years after the facility was constructed and placed in operation. The 65-year lease specified that "all structures and signs shall be so designed and placed as to detract as little as possible from the natural beauty of the surrounding area." It was a little late.

Kokee Park had no Secretary of the Interior to object. No Kokee park official had ventured to say "no," despite a feasibility report in which alternate suitable sites on Kauai were named and mapped, all meeting the Air Guard requirement of an unobstructed northern sweep from a high elevation. The alternate sites had no paved access road, however, and the Air National Guard was apparently unwilling to spend funds to construct their own access road to build at a site less harmful to natural scenic beauty and public areas of Kokee State Park.

Hawaii's fledgling State Park system welcomed its first director, Richard Dunlap, in 1960. He was greatly disturbed at the destruction along the rim of Kalalau Valley and at Kalalau Lookout, and when the Air National Guard began planning its annual field training at Kokee, and requested the exclusive use of organized group camp and housing facilities, Dunlap expressed concern and said in no uncertain terms that "the pri-

mary purpose of these facilities . . . are to accommodate people who come to the park for recreational purposes."

A year later, Haruo Shigazawa, a State Land Office employee, learned that the Guard was planning to construct a tropospheric communication facility next to their radar station at Kokee. In a hand written memo to Dunlap, he pleaded that no commitment be made at that time on negotiations for a proposed 65-year lease to the Guard, because the area they were proposing for the facility "includes a portion of Kalalau Lookout—the most significant recreational feature in Kokee Park."

Hirano Cook, head of the Board of Land and National Resources, opposed the request in a 1963 letter to the Army Engineers. It was the first time in anybody's memory that a high Territorial or State official had challenged the U. S. military in Hawaii. Cook explained the importance of Kalalau Lookout as "The principle recreational feature of this park" and asked that "adequate consideration be given to our park plans if military construction is absolutely essential." In subsequent discussions, it was disclosed that some of the military problems were financial and they could not afford to build long access roads to other sites. However, Cook insisted that every possible alternate location should be explored, and also suggested that the twenty-acre site be reduced in size so that any military expansion within the site would not be near the Lookout.

After thinking it over for one year and three months, the Air Guard decided the "absolutely essential" tropospheric facility was not needed in Kokee.

It was only a temporary victory for Cook. A second radar facility was being planned for Kauai. The Pacific Missile Range people, who already had space-tracking facilities on Hawaii and Oahu islands, announced that Kauai was being considered for a permanent tracking station to support Project Mercury. Commander Albert W. Hayward, Pacific Missile Range representative, diverted anticipated objections in a release to newsmen on October 28, 1959, asserting that "if Kauai is chosen, the Mana area will be the site." On December 9, Governor Quinn, in a public statement, also reaffirmed that the tracking station would be at Mana, near Barking Sands.

The military had long ago learned that the hand is quicker than the eye, and while publicly pointing to Mana, their engineers were conducting test borings at Kokee by the middle of November and had concluded electronic tests even before that date.

When the Navy first approached the Division of Forestry for a right of entry permit to drill test borings, they refused to reveal the location, saying it was "somewhere on Kauai in the mountains, so just sign the permit." It took almost thirty minutes to find out it was in Kokee. When asked why Kokee was chosen, they said nineteen other sites met the site criteria, but Kokee already had a road and was a developed area. The Navy representative added, "When we are finished, we'll use the facility for recreation cabins and a swimming pool." The military requested exclusive use of 95 acres of park and the Kokee Park headquarters area all in fee simple. They also mentioned in passing that all private cars and visitors would be banned from Kokee while the tracking facilities were in use. Rear Admiral Solomons said the 95 acres would provide "minimum space" and were required "to support the Pacific Missile Range in its contribution to the national defense program." Others were saying it was for the "man in space" program.

Wayne Collins, head of the Forestry Division, was shocked at the Navy's attitude and received Governor Quinn's support in opposing the uncompromising demands, which amounted to confiscation of Kokee State Park.

Meanwhile, Admiral Jack P. Monroe, Commanding Officer of the Pacific Missile Range, appeared at Kokee to inspect the tracking station site, and said the control building would be on Halemanu Hill, overlooking Waimea Canyon. He also affirmed that the "station will be permanent," and spoke glowingly of the $800,000 construction cost and fifty full-time employees.

Collins efforts at compromise were delaying the project, and two weeks later, newsmen still reported that the Navy was looking over "prospective sites." George Siu, acting Land Commissioner, visited Kauai and said, "The State intends to do everything in its power to cooperate with the Navy in establishing the proposed installations . . . the plans would be an assist to Kauai's economy . . . This department will see that local interests are protected, safeguarding the forest reserve and preserving the natural beauty of the area for tourists and local people."

Yielding to Collins arguments in support of Kokee Park's integrity, the Navy agreed that the tracking station only needed 16 acres instead of 95, and that it would be unnecessary to take over the ranger station or close the road. Collins had saved the park, but not without serious losses. Halemanu hill, ancient camp site of the feather collectors and once overgrown with wild tropical vegetation, was now a leveled acre, sprouting revolving corkscrew antennae.

Parks Director Dunlap sent a long list of damages to the State Land Office, saying, "The installation of the Pacific Missile Range facility resulted in unnecessary damage to recreational values and park improvements which could have been avoided." He specifically blamed "excessive tree trimming and removal of trees in the installation of electric power service . . . lack of screen (and) or excessive clearing of tree and shrub growth to achieve operational requirements." Hundreds of endemic koa trees, seedling sandalwood, and mature planted exotics had been chainsawed down along several miles of entrance road by power line construction crews.

Dunlap did not last long as Director of State Parks. His letter was filed and forgotten, and he returned to the mainland. The State Land Office failed to recognize or adequately support his belief that "if military installations are necessary in our parks, they should be located, constructed, and maintained on the basis that fair and just consideration be given to park values." It was a fair enough request. Few would disagree that this could be well accomplished by coordinated planning from the very beginning—including site selection.

The Navy continued encroaching on Kauai forest reserve and park lands. In the winter of 1964, Navy helicopters again buzzed over Napali-Kona forest reserve on what appeared to observers as reconnaisance flights over enemy territory. Occasionally, they landed on isolated ridges and installed portable electronic antennae and technical gear, generally folding everything up and flying off before dark. Surveymen were seen taping

the winding dirt road atop Makaha Ridge. Checks with the Territorial Forester revealed that no entry permits had been issued to anyone. Tom Tagawa, staff assistant to the State Forester, advised the Kauai forester to "stop trespassers from continuing further work." The Navy was notified and belatedly requested an entry permit.

The Navy letter must have been hand delivered with great urgency, for on the very next day, the State Board of Land and Natural Resources approved right of entry to the Navy—for surveys only. Regardless, the Navy began clearing Makaha Ridge immediately for construction of radar towers for the complex remote instrumentation facility, heedlessly bulldozing lands of the State forest reserve and the conservation district, land within the area recommended by the Secretary of the Interior for a Kauai National Park.

Kauai forester Ralph Daehler requested that, "If the military must install equipment in the forest reserve, it is my hope that it can be located at the end of a narrow ridge, such as Kaaweiki, where it will least interfere with . . . recreation." Neither the Navy nor the Land Board listened. It was the same story all over again. Despite objections of the Kauai forester, this time supported by Honolulu conservationists, the military was not to be stopped. Even personal pleas to the governor to investigate alternate sites were of no avail—it was argued that the project was in the national interest, and anyway, work had already started. Even Jim Ferry, Chairman of the State Land Board, when asked about the possible damage to NaPali, shrugged his shoulders, saying, "There is nothing I can do," although at the time a lease had not yet been granted by the Board.

At the regular December meeting of the Board of Land and Natural Resources, the Navy's Makaha lease request was discussed (no public hearing was required). Richard Cox, Chairman of the Conservation Council's land committee, testified that the "Council feels that such installation in the area will be aesthetically undesirable," and urged that suitable alternate sites be investigated before proceeding. Staff members of the Division of Forestry in attendance sat in silence, never mentioning the letter of their Kauai colleague opposing the site and suggesting that other sites be considered.

The Chairman of the Board said that he "personally visited the area recently and . . . the proposed location is rather barren and won't deter the hunting or forestry activities in the area." The Navy representative affirmed that the radar facility would be "below the top of the main ridge" and would not harm the scenic beauty of the area. That was enough for the Board. At the fall of the koa gavel, they unanimously approved the lease. Unknown to the Board, at the very time they were meeting bulldozers were already at work, shaving off the entire top of the lower ridge and pushing soil down the sides of adjacent Makaha Valley. The new lease specifically prohibited "waste, strip, or spoil" and specified that measures must be taken to "prevent damage to . . . geological features and related natural resources." The Navy had not waited to read the fine print.

Hawaii's Vice President of the Federation of Western Outdoor Clubs wrote Secretary of Defense Robert McNamara, suggesting that the Makaha project be relocated on a ridge less damaging to Kokee State Park.

The Navy replied for Mr. McNamara, with assurances that the "location was chosen after careful technical study because it is in sight of the airfield and is high enough to overlook and therefore operate effectively with the underwater range just offshore." Rear Admiral V. G. Lambert expressed confidence that the construction "will in no way mar the natural beauty of Makaha Ridge," though it already had. He ignored the fact that forester Daehler's alternate proposal for Kaaweiki Ridge would have placed the facility even closer to Barking Sands and the underwater range while still maintaining the desired altitude. A subsequent exchange of letters between the Navy in Washington and concerned conservationists in Honolulu only revealed further strangeness in Navy logic. When it was suggested that the Navy combine its facilities with the NASA Kokee tracking station, saving millions of dollars in construction costs, Admiral Lambert claimed that an "inversion layer" prevented use of radar above 2,000 feet, yet the joint Air Force-FAA radar facility atop 4,500 foot Mount Kaala on Oahu experienced little difficulty. When questioned, several FAA radar operators said they had no particular problems with any "inversion layer" and were mystified that anyone would consider it a problem in Hawaii.

All arguments failed and the Navy rolled on. The private contractor for the Navy quickly proceeded to construct sup-porting buildings and erected two sixty-foot radar towers on windswept Napali. The strong, bold cliffs, rising majestically 1,500 feet above the blue sea, once a landmark for the early Polynesian voyagers to Hawaii and later probably the first land seen through the ocean haze by Captain Cook, could no longer be a quiet resting place for hunters or hikers marveling at the vast, unbroken panorama.

The unique natural beauty of the Napali coast, once stretching without pause fifteen miles from Barking Sands to Haena, and viewed from the air by thousands of visitors every year—was irreparably broken at Makaha. The proposed National Park had lost one of its treasures.

Sunao Kido, Deputy Director of the Land Board, wrote Governor John Burns that "I am satisfied . . . that this Department has taken every reasonable precaution against any wanton destruction of Hawaii's natural beauty." Hawaii's new·State Park Director, Joseph Souza, once a ranger at Kokee, was quoted by Kido as saying "that no work on the ridge is visible from the highway." Kido could have gone further and said that no work was visible from Honolulu.

Rear Admiral Lambert, Chief of the Bureau of Naval Weapons, had the last word on the completed facilities, saying that their "usefulness in the interest of national defense should silence those who find them objectionable."

Kukui blossoms

10. Water

*Development of the resource that had made Kauai beautiful
and its agriculture rich, now became an issue, and the Bureau
of Reclamation offered its help—at an unknown cost.*

SOMETIMES HIDDEN in narrow slots of deep canyons, at other times dropping boldly in thousand-foot falls, Waimea River surged unobstructed to the sea sixty years ago. Wild Hawaiian ducks floated lightly on sometimes frothy, sometimes tea-colored water from Alakai Swamp, the river's source. The river scoured the cliffs of Waimea Canyon, and continued seaward, replenished on its way by numerous streams and springs draining clear water from the dike complex within the porous volcanic rock. Great quantities of storm water escaped freely from the wettest land on earth, flowing deep in this, the longest Hawaiian river.

As the river neared the sea, small diversion ditches carried water into taro patches and as quickly returned it to the river. The river's flow was maintained and neither in winter nor summer did the sand at the river mouth close across the stream. Waimea Village, embracing both sides of the river where it entered the sea, never flooded.

Hans Faye's artesian wells, scattered about the Mana plains, provided ample water for cane irrigation in these early pioneering days. As planting expanded and additional lands closer to Waimea were reclaimed, additional sources of water were required, and Faye investigated the possibility of bringing waters from Alakai Swamp, which was at a sufficiently high elevation for gravity irrigation of the Mana lowlands. His ideas were translated into a feasible ditch system by Kekaha Sugar Company engineers, and by 1910 Kekaha completed a small diversion structure at the junction of Koaie Stream nine miles upriver, in the heart of Waimea Canyon, diverting virtually all the summer flow of Waimea River into extensive, newly cultivated cane fields.

Within a few years after water was diverted from Waimea River, its physical appearance changed markedly. Trees and brush swiftly sprouted and grew in the dry channel when waters shrank to a trickle during summer months. Soil, sand, and rocks slid into the channel in spring freshets, and normal winter flows were no longer sufficient to clear the channel. Once ten feet deep for most of its length, the river became a sluggish, shallow stream, flowing between exposed lava boulders. At the river mouth, where small sailing schooners once anchored for provisions and fresh water in depths of over twenty feet, a permanent sand bar obstructed the river's entrance to the sea. The channel had plugged up. There was no longer a river reservoir to hold flood waters or to keep open a clear passage to the sea.

In 1912, Waimea Village was flooded for the first time in the villagers' memory, when the river overflowed during winter rains. Every year thereafter, the river crested dangerously, causing minor floods and constantly posing a threat to life and property in a village unprepared to cope with the rising waters. Eleven years after the Kekaha Ditch was completed, Waimea suffered severe losses in the most destructive flood ever to inundate a Kauai community. An act of man had changed an act of God into disaster.

After Kekaha successfully purchased its power plant and the Waimea diversion dam lands in the 1920 auction, management invested heavily in an elaborate system of small dams, ditches, and tunnels to skim off additional Waimea River water at its source in Alakai Swamp.

Roads were built by hand across Kokee and into Alakai. Camp Ten on Mohihi Stream became notorious as the coldest and wettest habitation on Kauai. With little mechanical equipment, miles of ditches and tunnels were pushed through the rock and clay rim of Waimea Canyon by pick and shovel. The rough construction crews lived on the land, and foraged all of Kokee for fish and game. Exotic plants were cultivated for food along the surveyed route and allowed to spread wild into the jungle as the tunnel crews advanced. Kokee cabins were broken into and hunting regulations violated in a lawless atmosphere reminiscent of railroad building in the wild west.

When the ditches and tunnels were completed in 1927, 1,000 acres were added to Kekaha's sugar production by the gravity water system, and work continued on the 1.7 billion gallon reservoir on Waiakoali Stream to hold water sufficient for another 2,000 acres of irrigated cane. The concrete dam core was poured and plans for clearing 100 acres of Alakai Swamp for the reservoir site prepared, when visiting senators expressed concern over construction of large reservoirs at the head of Waimea Canyon. They considered introducing bills requiring government approval of plans and specification to protect the residents of Waimea from possible failure of the dam with a reservoir filled to capacity. No concern was expressed for the rare flora and fauna threatened with destruction by sluicing out of Alakai Swamp the material for an 887-foot-long earthen dam.

Unforeseen engineering and political delays plagued Kekaha's construction timetable, and the dam and reservoir projects were abandoned because of the short time remaining on the lease. Depression fears postponed work again following the lease in 1938, and war clouds mothballed the project when plans were revived in 1940. After World War II, Kekaha hesitated again, awaiting a new lease, hopefully of longer duration. The delay was fatal to the private project.

Kauai Republican Senator Noburu Miyake introduced a resolution in 1949 memorializing Congress to develop water storage facilities at Alakai Swamp for irrigation and production of hydroelectric power. Kekaha manager Lindsay Faye pleaded that if the lease were renewed, the plantation would be willing to construct the original irrigation reservoir project with private financing. Faye asked the Territory to grant a longer lease and a subsidy in form of reduced land rental for 15 years.

But the Territorial government, now no longer completely under planter influence, pulled the rug out from under Kekaha in renewing the lease and cancelled all water privileges Kekaha had previously enjoyed. Water development rights were transferred to the Territory and made available to Kekaha under terms of a water license. Fifty years of private water development in Kekaha-Kokee came to an end as the new postwar politicians moved government into active management of water resources and created the Hawaii Irrigation Authority.

Government control of water could have been a good thing. The government could have established a program of water development in the best interests of the land and of all the people of Kauai, but it did not. Kekaha Sugar's threat to Kokee and Alakai Swamp was nothing compared to the threat soon posed by the U. S. Bureau of Reclamation.

A special Congressional committee of the House Interior and Insular Affairs Committee came to Kauai in 1954 for public hearings and Senator Miyake followed their visit with a letter to Public Lands Commissioner Marguerite Ashford, asking her to initiate an investigation of the possibilities of government participation in an Alakai Swamp reservoir. Miyake had apparently forgotten the Territorial law he had authored which specifically limited the Irrigation Authority to projects serving "small-scale farms," except for the right to sell water in excess of the needs of the farms within a project. The 15,000 acres of Hawaiian Homes Commission lands in the mountains southwest of Kokee offered opportunities for homesteading to small farmers, but would use only a small portion of the water available from a major irrigation project. Officials also ignored the fact that Hawaiian Homes commissioners had no plans for use of its upper Kekaha lands, nor had any investigation been made of their suitability for agriculture. Nevertheless, the 1955 Legislature directed that a study be made for a public irrigation project in Kokee, although the only known beneficiary was Kekaha

Sugar, which for three decades had attempted to construct an irrigation reservoir and dam with its own funds.

Findings of the 1957 Irrigation Authority report to Republican Governor Samuel Wilder King should have discouraged proponents of the project. The report stated "that it would not be practicable to incorporate either flood control or hydroelectric power development in the plans for the proposed Kokee irrigation project," and went on to say that "since the project area is isolated from the Honolulu market, a relatively low cost of production would be required to offset the high transportation costs. . . . There is inadequate information to show that crops can be grown under irrigation in the service area at a sufficient profit to the homesteaders to insure the financial success of a project."

The chief engineer of the Authority did find, however, "that it would be feasible to construct a somewhat limited project to provide the additional supply of water needed for optimum irrigation of cane on the 2,200 acres of government land now leased by the Kekaha Sugar Company." He believed the cost of water for cane irrigation to be within acceptable economic limits.

Ignoring their own adverse report, the Irrigation Authority recommended that the Legislature appropriate $250,000 to make detailed engineering and geological investigations of a project they had concluded was economically unsound. Kauai Representative Allen Ezell supported the Authority, and introduced a resolution to make the Kokee project eligible for Federal funds under the Small Reclamation Projects Act of 1956. The Bureau of Reclamation, ever anxious to expand its sphere of influence, jumped into the act.

Floyd E. Dominy, Commissioner of the Bureau of Reclamation, collaborating with the State Division of Water and Land Development, authored a "Kokee water project" report. Even Dominy recognized the improbability of any diversified farming on Hawaiian Homes lands "because of the many economic uncertainties and technological problems involved." The feasibility of the irrigation portion of the project was based entirely on the assumption that all the water would be devoted to sugar cane production, assuming, of course, that Kekaha would buy water at the asking price.

The value of the Kokee dam to Kauai was proven largely illusionary in the report, although Kauai politicians kept up their claims of more jobs, more farms, and cheaper power. In actuality, the project would offer few new jobs, no economically practical small farms, and might actually raise the cost of consumer power on Kauai for the next 50 years.

The $19,450,000 project would be financed mostly by a Federal loan, to be repaid in 50 years at three per cent interest. Direct benefits of any consequence to Kauai would come only during the four years of construction as payrolls circulated fresh money into the depressed island economy.

The hydroelectric power plant was designed to provide power only at peak loads. There would be insufficient water to run the turbines at the design rate for more than a few hours a day without draining the reservoir. Existing steam plants would have to continue to operate and new plants would continue to be built as demands increase. Kekaha would be unable to use all the water at peak flows even in the dry summer months, and the

surplus water could only be flushed into the sea. In winter months even less water, or sometimes none at all, would be required to satisfy sugar irrigation needs. To expect Kekaha to pay for water it cannot use would be unreasonable, but it was an assumption important to the justification of the dam.

Cost of hydroelectric power is estimated as being at least equal to cost of producing power with steam generators fired by oil and presently unused cane waste bagasse. It was claimed that Kauai Electric Company, the private public power utility on Kauai, would be able to build a conventional power plant at Port Allen for $2.5 million, using private capital, and supply power to Kauai at a much cheaper rate than proposed in the hydroelectric project.

Flood control benefits would be negligible, and the small farms the dam was supposed to make possible are not needed in Hawaii. Oceanic Properties, land development subsidiary of Castle and Cooke, one of the nation's largest food processors, reported to the State Land Use Commission in 1963 that, contrary to general opinion, "Availability of additional land is not a major factor in determining the amount of truck crops now grown or that will be grown in the future." According to Oceanic Properties, "If the 550 acres now used for truck crops on Oahu were fully used, . . . Oahu could produce *all* the truck crops it needs for its 1970 population without importing any from the neighbor islands." Oceanic stated that small farmers could not compete with the mainland in growing major truck crops.

In the entire State of Hawaii, only 1,300 acres are used for diversified farming. Should all the proposed 1,600 acres in upper Kekaha be put into successful truck crop production, by small farmers or by an efficient large agricultural company, it would mean economic ruin to every small truck farmer in the State. It is difficult to believe that supporters of the Kokee project would advocate something so economically undesirable.

The Bureau figured the benefit-cost ratio at 1.44 to 1.00. Even this low index was obtained by computing power revenues 22 per cent higher than current power rates and adding water revenues from Kekaha Sugar based upon year-round averages—whether Kekaha used the water or not. Either the people of Kauai would pay more for power, or Kekaha would pay more for water. Both parties will undoubtedly resist higher payments, although negotiations with Kekaha on their new lease expiring in 1968 place Kekaha in a poor bargaining position. The Bureau may well find his benefit-cost ratio at zero and the Federal loan to Kauai a grant unless the people of Kauai are willing to pay more for power and Kekaha accepts lower profits. Neither eventuality appears likely.

One hundred and fifty acres of Alakai Swamp adjacent to the botanically important Lehua Makanoe bog may be stripped to a depth of twenty feet to provide fill for the proposed half mile long earth dam on Kawaikoi Stream. A six-acre rock quarry blasted from the rim of Waimea Canyon will provide lava riprap. A second dam is proposed on Mohihi Stream, deep within Alakai Swamp, to divert additional water into a canal one mile long, penetrating untouched swamp country. The proposed reservoir will flood more than 400 acres of the Alakai Swamp Wilderness Preserve, and coupled with strip mining for fill

material, hauling roads, and construction camps, will ruin perhaps one thousand acres of unique American swamp land. The irreplaceable flora and fauna are not represented in the Kokee project's "benefit-cost" index, and are by no means replaced by the recreation value of a reservoir estimated to fluctuate over 150 feet in depth, denuding the shoreline of all vegetation. Little boating or fishing recreation, in any case, could be enjoyed at the reservoir site which is only a few miles from the wettest spot on earth and where rainfall reaches 150 inches in some years. Even swimming would be unlikely due to the cold water and its uninviting brown color.

The Board of Land and Natural Resources set aside 9,939 acres of Alakai Swamp as a wilderness preserve on January 24, 1964, yet the Kokee Water Project Report, released later in the year, does not recognize the preserve's existence. The preserve is an important one. Several species of native perching birds, found only in Alakai Swamp, are becoming very rare. Most significant of these are the o-o, the Kauai akialoa, nukupuu, the anianiau, and the puaiohi, or Kauai thrush, all members of a unique Hawaiian family of birds which are nearly extinct. The birds are dependent on undisturbed native forest, and the proposed reservoir site intrudes upon their principal habitat. Recreation motorboat noises and the dieback following land clearing and trail building in the tropical jungle may result in total loss of birds found nowhere else on earth. Mountain streams such as Kawaikoi and its tributaries, are used year-round by the Koloa, a rare native Hawaiian duck, which might find a fish-stocked, boat-filled reservoir quite inhospitable.

Napali

11. The Land Law

*A voice for the land, for so long just a whisper in Hawaii, was
finally heard, and a land ethic began to become part of the law.*

WHEN HAWAIIAN statehood arrived, no island
county possessed a comprehensive zoning ordinance.
Even Honolulu's zoning procedures were riddled
with variances obtained virtually on request, as individual landowners changed land uses to produce the most profitable return
in the shortest time. Producing pineapple fields were converted
to memorial park cemeteries. Sugar-cane acreage became urban
sprawl. Planning for schools, water and fire protection was in
disorder, and rising county administrative and public service
costs were reflected in higher taxes. Every new subdivision was
recorded as a net loss to the county—the new land taxes never
equaled rising county expenses. Hawaii's sugar and pineapple
industries, already threatened by low-cost competition from
overseas, were soon faced with the choice of yielding land for
urban use or paying prohibitive taxes to retain the land in
agriculture.

Clearly, the limited land of Hawaii was not being managed
in the long-term best interests of the state. To satisfy the needs
of Hawaii's people, then and for the future, the first general plan
prepared by any state was presented to the first elected Governor
of Hawaii with great fanfare in January 1961. The much-
heralded general plan proposed that the state prepare to meet
increasing demands for public services and improvements, stimulate capital formation and private investment by creating the
proper "investment climate," and attempt to balance the distribution of population and economic activity among the five main
islands. Its goals were not to be realized, nor was the plan
adopted by any island county. The general plan was an administrative and planning failure from the beginning, and few of its
recommendations were ever implemented. The far-reaching
proposal crumbled in the face of opposition from provincial
island politicians, small landowners, and land speculators crowding Hawaii on the heels of the plentiful mortgage money which
arrived with statehood. Mainlanders and local real estate operators, searching for quick investment opportunities in the new,

prosperous state, saw the document as a block to short-term
speculative gains.

The General Plan was abandoned by the new State Democratic administration. The goals of the General Plan, although
visionary at the time and politically unworkable, did provide
the basis for a state land use law, which outlived the General
Plan failure and successfully overcame carefully laid political
attempts to relegate it, also, to the political graveyard of progressive legislation.

Born of the new Democratic Legislature, Hawaii's unique
Land Use Law owes its life to the sugar and pineapple planters,
who saw new threats to their industry posed by urban sprawl,
rising land taxes, and speculative manipulation of agricultural
lands. Many years before, the industry had saved their watersheds from ruin by financing a reforestation program, beneficial
to all Hawaii. Now, Hawaii's major corporations joined forces
with the progressive Democratic legislature to overwhelm county
government opposition and, with bi-partisan votes, established
the first statewide zoning law in the nation. Act 187, "relating
to the zoning powers of the State and the assessment of real
property based upon zones established by the State," became
law on July 11, 1961.

The legislature described its purpose in creating Act 187:
Inadequate controls have caused many of Hawaii's limited and valuable lands to be used for purposes that may have a short-term gain to a
few but result in a long-term loss to the income and growth potential
of our economy. Inadequate bases for assessing lands according to
their value in those uses that can best serve both the well-being of the
owner and the well-being of the public have resulted in inequities in
the tax burden, contributing to the forcing of land resources into uses
that do not best serve the welfare of the State. Scattered subdivisions
with expensive, yet reduced, public services; the shifting of prime
agricultural lands into non-revenue producing residential uses when
other lands are available that could serve adequately the urban needs;
failure to utilize fully multiple-purpose lands; these are evidences of
the need for public concern and action. Therefore, the Legislature
finds that in order to preserve, protect and encourage the development

of the lands in the State for those uses to which they are best suited for the public welfare and to create a complementary assessment basis according to the contribution of the lands in those uses to which they are best suited, the power to zone should be exercised by the State and the methods of real property assessment should encourage rather than penalize those who would develop these uses.

A State Land Use Commission was established, with members from each senatorial district appointed by the Governor and confirmed by the senate.

The first Commission met immediately to initiate the herculean task of districting all state lands. Staff was hired and public hearings scheduled on all islands. The apparent legislative intent of the law, to protect prime agricultural land, was given first consideration. All existing forest reserves were placed in "conservation," and land in residential and industrial use (including military) along with subdivided lots of record, was districted "urban." All land remaining was designated "agriculture."

As the 1962 legislators settled into their seats in Iolani Palace, it became evident that opponents would attempt to block confirmation of Governor William Quinn's appointees to the Land Use Commission before they could adopt and make legal the temporary boundaries. As expected, the Senate refused to confirm the Commission, but not until after the boundaries had become legal.

After the senators flew home, Governor Quinn appointed a new Commission. This second commission used a Federal urban planning grant to hire a private planning consultant to make recommendations for the permanent boundaries. Extensive public hearings and preparation of guidelines and regulations were also undertaken by the second Commission, but to no avail. Governor John Burns, a Democrat, defeated Quinn in a close election and the new Democratic majority in the Senate failed to confirm Quinn's appointees. The second Commission's permanent boundaries were never adopted. Governor Burns appointed a third Land Use Commission, and the work of determining permanent boundaries started again.

Following 29 public hearings and 30 Commission meetings on all the islands, the Commission completed zoning of all lands. The resulting maps constitute not only a general plan for Hawaii's population growth and development, but are an inventory of its natural scenic resources, park lands, wilderness, and beach reserves, all included in a conservation district. The permanent boundaries were enacted into law in August, 1964.

All land in the State of Hawaii, public and private, was zoned into four districts: urban, rural, agricultural, and conservation. The boundaries of every city, town, and populated area were determined by the Commission. Within these urban areas, county zoning ordinances and regulations prevail.

Rural districts, by law, were composed of small farms and low-density residential areas. The Commission, in determining rural zones, created new "rural subdivisions" of half-acre lots, but maintained the intended character of farmlike country residential communities.

Agricultural districts included all farming activities, ranging from ancient Hawaiian taro patches still in production to diversified truck crop farming and large sugar and pineapple plantations. Sugar-mill and industrial activities ancillary to agriculture production were also zoned agriculture.

Conservation districts were considered by the first two Commissions as little more than a catchall for lands not classifiable as urban or agriculture. The third Commission placed conservation districts on an equal level with urban zones and, following careful deliberations, rezoned substantial areas of urban and agricultural lands into conservation classifications. Many private ranch lands were placed as nonconforming uses in the conservation district to give legal significance to their great natural beauty. All of Kalalau Valley, a working cattle ranch, was zoned conservation.

The Commission established by regulation a policy that all land with a slope steeper than 20 per cent would be placed in conservation, primarily to protect the remaining tropical green ridges sloping upward from the hillside residential communities of Honolulu. Hawaii conservationists supported the Commission in these controversial decisions, and their influence was important in converting the basically agricultural law into an instrument of positive preservation and protection of Hawaii's natural scenic resources.

The Land Use Law directed inclusion in the conservation district of all lands necessary for protection of "watersheds and water sources, forests, scenic areas, parks, wilderness and beach preserves, conserving endemic plants, fish and wildlife, preventing floods and soil erosion, and other related activities not detrimental to a multiple-use conservation concept."

Hawaii's Trail and Mountain Club outlined the first proposed conservation areas for the Commission. The Scenic Resources committee of the Conservation Council for Hawaii, under the author's chairmanship, prepared the first actual inventory of Hawaii's natural scenic resources and delineated in detail all land areas of conservation importance. Representatives of the Council testified at numerous public hearings of the Land Use Commission and presented the conservationists' arguments for including all lands of scenic significance in the conservation district. It was the independent conservationists who convinced the Commission that the law should be used to protect scenic beauty, as well as sugar and pineapple lands. They argued that both are of equal importance to the state's economy and deserve equal protection.

Governor Burns had urged this understanding when, in one of his first post-election public statements to the Conservation Council, he said, "We have the basic land use laws on our books to protect and enhance Hawaii's resources of scenic beauty and open spaces . . . Ownership of land does not carry with it the right to deface its natural beauty in the name of progress."

12. Prospects

FOR ALL THE neglect and abuse of its past, the land of Kauai remains the most beautiful in Hawaii. Between the dunes of Barking Sands and the summit of Mount Waialeale, the wettest spot on earth, lie one hundred square miles of spectacular parkland: palis dropping half a mile to the Pacific Ocean surf; hidden valleys a thousand feet deep and a rock throw wide; rolling hills covered with red-blossomed ohia lehua; delightful walking trails at the edge of Alakai Swamp—a wilderness brightened with rare plants and with bird songs heard nowhere else in the world.

Dramatic variations in weather occur within the area. The five thousand foot summit of Mount Waialeale on the eastern boundary averages 500 inches of rain per year, and one year 950 inches were recorded, yet only seventeen miles to the west, arid Barking Sands receives a scant 20 inches. The vegetation varies accordingly, and the hundred square miles is a botanist's paradise.

The gracefully fluted cliffs of Napali rise directly from the blue Pacific to elevations of 2,000 to 3,000 feet. The spectacle of the coastline culminates in Kalalau Valley where the stone

ruins of Hawaiian villages, ancient at the time of Captain Cook yet still populated fifty years ago, lie buried beneath lush tropical growth. The nearly vertical cliffs enclosing the valley are alternately revealed and obscured by shifting clouds carried on tropical trade winds, and occasionally the Specter of the Brocken appears on the moving mist.

The broad sweep of white coral sand at Barking Sands ends abruptly at Polihale Springs where the pali rises from the sea. For fifteen miles Napali continues, sliced sharply by deep, narrow valleys, many inaccessible except from small boats in the summer, or by helicopter. Deep volcanic browns are broken only by the occasional green of grass, until the more verdant amphitheater of Kalalau provides water for the bright leaves of mango fruit and kukui nut. Farther on, at Hanakapiai and Limahili, a misty jungle softness darkens the trees clinging to steep walls. At Hanakoa a two-thousand-foot string of white water drops from the pali top and then twists along the valley floor beneath groves of mountain apple trees.

The heart of the land is Alakai Swamp. Streams from the swamp rise and fall with the rain but pour all year long over rocky waterfalls into Waimea and Wainiha Canyons. Alakai is twenty miles of wilderness bog, rich in species of sedges, violets, and lobelias found nowhere else in the world.

Three species of birds; the Kauai creeper, the akialoa, and the nukupuu are found only in Alakai. They persist precariously, in constant danger of extinction from environmental alteration and introduction of alien plants. In the deep gorge of Waimea Canyon, the rare koloa maoli, or Hawaiian ducks, float on the slower pools, where noisy females can be heard quacking above the sound of the water. Once common throughout Hawaii, the small brown duck is now seen only in Waimea Canyon and on Niihau.

In Waimea Canyon the island's geological history is exposed in desert colors of orange-red cinder and brown decomposed lava, interrupted by bright green gulches of kukui. Waimea River is a sparkling chain 2,500 feet below the canyon rim. Along the canyon edges grow the Kauai greensword; on drier slopes grow the native white hibiscus tree, the only fragrant hibiscus. Thirty endemic lobelias can be found, including one with unusual blue flowers, and sandalwood is returning. Palms are scattered throughout the native forest, along with passion fruit, wild plums, and apples. Introduced trees grow well, including Japanese pine, cypress, silver oak, and redwood. Wild boar and goat bring the thrill of wildlife to the quiet jungle and windswept palis, and mokihana is here to make into the most fragrant lei of all.

The natural beauty of Kauai is only part of its appeal. The legends and stories of Hawaiian oral literature have endured here and on the other islands as few American Indian legends have endured in the continental United States. The aboriginal population of the islands, where land was limited, was heavier than anywhere on the mainland, and the land is more strongly imbued with the spirit of the native people. On Kauai, where the land is wildest, the native tradition is most intact. Every valley, cave, mountain and stream has its story.

One of the caves at Haena was the home of a dragon. He was a dragon with taste, and he chose a good spot. From the base of the Haena cliffs the view of the beach is excellent, and the beaches at Haena are among the most beautiful in the world. The producers of *South Pacific* shared the dragon's delight in them and chose Haena as the location for their movie.

There are three caves at Haena. The "dry" cave is at the base of the vertical cliffs behind Haena beach and its entrance is almost hidden in a forest of Java plum and kukui trees. It's a huge cave with a broad arched roof and vaulted chambers, and it would seem an ideal shelter from evening rains. Campers have discovered, however, that mosquitos from all over Kauai use it for that purpose. Sleeping in the rain is easier on the skin.

Once, long ago when savage battles were fought between rival chiefs of Kauai, an entire native army is said to have been imprisoned in the cave by hostile soldiers, who walled up the entrance. The prisoners were slowly starved to death, except for a young warrior who discovered a small opening through the cave roof and escaped to find aid. He returned too late. His former companions were all dead and the enemy was celebrating with savage orgies on the grounds of the present park pavillion.

Farther along the narrow country road to Ke'e Beach are two "wet" caves. On the floor of the first is a shallow and innocent pool. On the floor of the second, another pool, this one the home of the dragon. The water of this second pool is perfectly transparent and reflects the dim light from the cave's entrance, but it was not always so. Before 1898 the pool was covered with a yellow scum, a scum formed of the scales shed from the dragon's back. The dragon had its lair in the depths of the cavern, and anyone foolish enough to swim in the cool water would surely be seized. Today the scum is gone. The surface has been clear since the annexation of the Hawaiian Islands by the United States. The dragon, a loyal one, could not endure the domination of an alien race, and it departed for a far island where no white man has ever set foot.

The Hawaiian explanation for the red water of Alakai Swamp is as colorful as the explanation for the yellow scum at Haena Cave. I heard it on my first trip into Alakai.

My guide on the trip was Fred Taniguchi, a Robinson ranch cowboy and Japanese-Hawaiian son of Puakini, a famous Kauai guide familiar with every ridge of the Napali-Kona forest reserve. Loading our gear in Taniguchi's front yard at Waimea, we started off at dawn and spent the first day on horseback. It was a hot, dusty ride to our overnight stop at the old CCC camp on Waialae Stream. Here Kauai Forester Duval had planted the first redwood trees. They formed a small grove near the main building and were easily 75 feet tall, casting long shadows in the late afternoon sun. We expressed mixed feelings at finding the huge strangers, already many times taller than endemic ohia lehua trees, in the midst of our Hawaiian forest. Our thoughts were quickly diverted, however, when one of our group discovered exotic plum trees nearby, the branches bent almost to the ground with ripe purple fruit. Few native Hawaiian trees taste as good.

The next day we were up again in the chilly dawn air, and started out on horseback into a forest filled with birds and huge ohia. We crossed and recrossed Waialae Stream, which flowed full with red-brown water from Alakai. Occasionally, I reached down and plucked red thimble berries from along the trail or aimed my camera to snap masses of white ginger. Their deep

fragrance stayed with us long after the blossoms disappeared from view and we began to climb the steep switchback trail out of Waialae Valley into Alakai Swamp.

I asked Taniguchi how much farther we could go on horseback and he said we would know when we had gone far enough. We plodded onward into the swamp, the horses sinking deeper into the gray muck. Suddenly my horse lunged forward as he stepped across a fallen tree. His front legs dropped into the clay without meeting resistance and his belly hung over the vine-covered log. Taniguchi dismounted, slopped his way over to my frightened horse and said, "This is far enough." I left like a horse myself as I stumbled on foot deeper into the swamp, sinking with each step in the quagmire of a thousand years of rain.

One of the myraid small streams flowing from the top of Waialeale through this area has one of those unbelievably long Hawaiian names; *Ehaehaekamanuekanealohikealemaineikawai*, which in our language means, "Tear the bird, Kanealohi, the water is rippling." It refers to the tea-colored, sometimes reddish-brown water draining from Alakai Swamp. The scientific staff attached to the State Division of Forestry believes that the red color is caused by the Amaumau fern, growing in many areas of Kokee and Alakai. The Hawaiians have a more reasonable explanation. They tell the story of Princess Komalio, daughter of the high chief of Waimea, who was loved by Mano, a demigod. She failed to appreciate the honor and spurned his attentions. He kept at his courting, however, and one day he appeared in disguise at Waimea, in a canoe, announcing that he was a chief from another island. Even then she did not favor him, as she disliked his shifting and unsteady gaze—a "bad eye" she explained.

Failing to win her confidence, Mano decided he would have to use force to get her to his mountain lair. He changed himself into a great bird, and flew to the home of Komalio in Waimea. Finding her alone and sleeping in the garden, he seized her in his powerful talons and carried her to his cave near the headwaters of Waialae Stream. As he changed back into his ordinary form and lifted her sleeping body toward his lair under a waterfall, several drops of water fell on her face. She awoke, became frightened, and started to struggle. Mano lost his temper, killed Komalio, and buried her body by the side of Waialea Stream.

Since then, every time it rains in Alakai Swamp, the water runs through her grave, and the streams beneath it are red with her blood until they drop over the rim of Waimae Canyon.

There are two rocks between Nualolo and Awaawapuhi Valleys that have an origin as unhappy as the origin of Alakai's red water. The Hawaiians were a lighthearted people, but they appreciated tragedy, and most of the phenomena of their world had tragic explanations.

The two rocks are high on a talus ridge above what used to be the trail. They somewhat resemble humans climbing up the narrow ledges, and indeed they were once human, or superhuman. Their story is this: One of the powerful demigods who ruled the island, Naiwi by name, lived on the tops of ridges along this coast with his family, which included two children. One of the regular duties of the children was to climb down the cliff to the beach, fill their calabashes with water from a spring famous for its sweetness, and return to the top before dawn. The children, like most demigods, went out only at night, for daylight was fatal to them. They were children, however, and sometimes loitered on the way, playing pranks along the pali or stopping at some convenient flat spot for a game. One morning they became so engrossed in their play that they failed to notice the brightening sky to the east. When they finally saw it, they scrambled up the ridge as fast as they could climb, but succeeded only in reaching a point on the ridge just below the sheltering home caves. As they climbed over the last pinnacle before reaching the friendly shade of the mountain they were overtaken by the first deadly rays of sunlight, and instantly turned to stone. The two children stand on the pali today, the undelivered calabashes of water still on their backs, a lesson to all children on heeding the warnings of their parents.

The Hawaiians left more than just stories and ghosts on Kauai—they left tangible things; temples, house platforms, and terraces. Of sensible design to begin with, they are in disrepair now, their edges and angles softened by time and weather. There is nothing in them out of harmony with the land, and coming upon one while walking on Kauai is one of the fascinations of the island.

There is one temple, on Mount Waialeale, that still receives offerings. I camped near it several years ago, eager to try out a new tent I had bought in a mountain shop on the mainland. Waialeale, the rainiest place on earth, would be the ultimate test for my tent.

Visitors to the summit of Waialeale usually use Keaku cave for shelter, and I ate dinner there, but the cave is always cold and damp and I was happy to brave the rain and pitch my tent. I crawled in for a cozy night, listening to the rain splattering lightly against the cotton tent walls, confident that I was camping in as wet a place as anybody had ever camped in before. I listened as the rain increased in intensity, and felt around anxiously for any leaks. The rain falling on the taut sides became louder and louder. The tent was soon like the inside of a bass drum. The noise became almost unbearable, but I was not about to leave the tent, and although I did not have a moment's sleep that night, not a drop of water entered the tent.

Near where I pitched camp on the summit, the Wainiha River, which flows into the Pacific Ocean on the north shore, has its source in a small lake. Held sacred by the early Hawaiians, it is hardly a real lake, only thirty feet in diameter and two feet deep in a rainstorm, which is almost always. The lake bottom is composed of small pebbles and sand and the water is clear, in contrast to the surrounding muck and stubby grass. Near the lake is a small temple platform of hand-fitted rock about ten feet square. It is the heiau of Waialeale, to which the Hawaiians of all classes once toiled from Hanalei and Waimea to pay homage to the gods of the woods and mountains.

That morning I walked toward the temple. The wet earth around the heiau platform sparkled with shiny dimes and nickels scattered there—present-day offerings still made to the gods of the mountain. Amazed at my own stupidity, I realized that I had forgotten to make my offerings the night before. Fortunately, the gods of Waialeale were not as powerful that night as they once had been, and they only deprived me of my sleep.

The head gods of the mountain, like the Haena dragon, may have departed in disgust, but Waialeale still dominates the island. For me it has always been, even more than the swamp, the most fascinating place on Kauai. Nowhere in the world is weather—the primeval power of cloud and rain—so dramatically on display. Camping on Waialeale is an experience like no other —not even approached in the Cascades of the northwest or in any other wet place in the continental United States.

Keaku Cave is the only dry place within a dozen miles of Waialeale. Perched high on the side of a clay cliff near a small stream that lower down becomes the Olokole River, the small cave, not high enough for a standing five-footer, is deep enough to stretch out in, though tenants must roll up their sleeping bags to cook dinner. The cave is one mile and three hours from the Waialeale summit, which though it is not the highest point on the mountain, is the most comfortable high point. Kawaikini peak, ninety feet higher and three-fifths of a mile south is too small and slippery to stand on.

The small stream is a hundred feet below the cave, but water needs are easily satisfied. We held a pan outside the cave entrance into the steady rain and filled it up in minutes with fresh, cold water. Far back in a dark corner of the cave is a crumbling wood calabash, undoubtedly brought here by a Hawaiian many years ago. We once found a rusting ship's lantern resting on the smooth, worn surface of the cave floor, but it fell into small pieces when we picked it up.

A native lapalapa tree stretches its slender branches across the cave entrance, shivering as its leaves catch the light breezes. The rare tree, growing only at high altitudes in Hawaiian swamps, has white wood that burns when it's green. Hula girls in the old days were called *Olapas* because they wiggled so much.

The tree offers a good perch for island birds, and curious over the rare visit of humans, they flock there. Birds seen nowhere else in the world are silhouetted against the overcast sky, perched on the mossy branches, singing unfamiliar calls and seemingly oblivious to the rain pouring from everything. Most noticeable is the bright scarlet liwi bird with its long curved beak, a beak especially suited for gathering nectar from ohia lehua and the rare lobelia blossoms that grow like parasites on it. Occasionally a green leaf will flutter gracefully away—an unknown bird camouflaged for the rain forest. The Akikiki or Kauai creeper chirps constantly in the cold, wet air, enjoying the rain and human visitors alike.

Once I got lost on a photographic expedition to Waialeale with Dick Davis, who was carrying most of my camera gear. We had been chopping our way through the featureless jungle, finding no sign of the summit trail, when Dick suddenly stopped swinging his machete, and called me to look. Straight ahead of us was the fresh path we had cut not an hour before. We had tramped in a circle and were lost.

Our predicament was serious, and we immediately climbed a tree to see what there was to see. The sky was overcast and misty. Every tree was the same height and all we looked into were the upper branches of more trees. The old boy scout trick of finding north from the side of the tree growing moss didn't work here. Moss several inches thick grew all around the slender branches I held on to, and when I squeezed a new branch it squirted like a clam.

We held still, watching the sensitive Lapalapa respond to the slight breezes, and after a half hour we agreed on the direction the wind was blowing. We stared at the rain clouds for minutes at a time, turning our heads to what we thought was the brightest spot in the darkness. We didn't notice any birds on the ground, but as we waited silently in the tree they flew over to look at us, perching within arm's reach on the wet branches.

Acting upon a unanimous vote, we decided the direction we should go, and set out again. We had a map but no compass, and the map was virtually worthless because we were not quite sure where we had started out from. Eventually we stumbled upon a stream we had encountered on our way in, and we retraced our steps back to camp. We returned considerably more aware of the danger of overconfidence in the Kauai wilderness.

Part of my own fascination for Waialeale is perhaps because of the trouble the mountain has caused me as a photographer. Waialeale has surprises for anyone dedicated enough to consider shooting pictures in the one hundred per cent humidity of the place. An underwater camera would actually be ideal for the trip—if you are satisfied with only one lens. Those who like a little versatility are stuck with conventional equipment—and a frustrating experience.

When my lens gets dirty on Waialeale, I give up for the day —I'm never able to wipe it. If I pull out a sheet of lens tissue it instantly absorbs moisture from the saturated air and disintegrates before my eyes. If in desperation I try a hankerchief, it becomes soaking wet before I'm ready to wipe. Should I go ahead anyway, the tiny droplets of water are only rearranged across the lens surface. The lens will not dry off until I get to the Primus store back in camp and some hot air. Sometimes a hidden dry handkerchief is the only solution.

Carrying an umbrella is, of course, ridiculous in this jungle. A raincoat shuts out the cooling air, and perspiration inside generally keeps you just as wet as the outside and very uncomfortable. Most hikers on Waialeale wear an old shirt and get wet. I generally keep warm as long as I'm walking, and reserve a dry shirt in the pack to pull out for lunch. Cameras hang on a neck strap underneath my shirt. Taking a picture, I unbutton my shirt, lean over to keep the rain out, take off the lens cap, snap the shutter and immediately cover everything. Any rain on the lens ends photography for the day, and a lens cap is mandatory.

For a time exposure, I extend the tripod legs full length and screw on my camera. If I just stand the tripod out in the swamp mud, it slowly disappears from sight. Sometimes I'm able to make time exposures down around ankle level. My trick is to search for exposed root clusters spaced equally apart on three sides and carefully spot the tripod accordingly. After pulling the tripod out of the mud, I check to see if the rubber tips are still in place. They generally are not.

Probably the most difficult problem for the photographer with a 35mm camera occurs when he finishes exposing the roll and flips the knob for rewinding the film back into the cartridge. It won't go back. Not even a little bit. The film base gradually soaks up moisture and swells inside the camera box. It simply gets too fat to go back in the can.

The only solution I've found is to switch to another camera. After dark, back in camp, I crawl head first into my sleeping

bag, open the camera, disassemble the metal cartridge and wind the film back in by hand.

Waialeale has a more unusual challenge than common mountains of rock and ice. Camping on it can be trying, but epidermis is waterproof, and once you're used to it, rain can be refreshing. Bill Hardy, who climbed the mountain twenty-two times between 1911 and 1920, clearly couldn't get enough of Waialeale's rain on his face or its mud between his toes. For the old Hawaiian priests, for Bill Hardy and for me Waialeale is a beautiful and completely satisfactory central point for the land of Kauai.

It is a land that deserves preservation, a more certain protection than the State of Hawaii has the resources or ability to supply. No appropriate state agency has taken action to guard against the continued stripping of the Napali reef and shore of shellfish and other sea life. Helicopter loads of collectors have descended on Milolii Beach and departed with almost every live, mature shell living on the reef there. Helicopters fly on call into every valley and beach of isolated Napali, carrying in hunters and campers alike, under no flight or landing restrictions, without obtaining concession rights through public bidding procedures—as provided by law—or making payments of any kind for commercial use of State land.

The State Division of Parks included in its 1965 budget money for the construction of a new Waimea Canyon lookout and improved picnic grounds at Puukapele, and these would have been excellent additions to the Kokee State Park, but instead the Board of Land and Natural Resources, over the objections of the acting Chief of Parks, voted a right-of-entry permit at Puukapele to construct a heliport for three helicopters scheduled to land and take off over Waimea rim every fifteen minutes.

When the Air Force insisted that a radar station be built on the summit of Haleakala, Hawaii National Park denied them the site. The State was unwilling to resist the same demands on Kokee.

The State Land Use Law provides that special approval be granted for all land uses within the conservation district, and requires that all construction be harmonious with the environment. The State Land Board, in issuing a right-of-entry permit to the Navy on Makaha Ridge and permitting construction of radar facilities prior to approval or imposition of design, clearly violated the intent of its own regulations.

Neither the Division of State Parks nor the Division of Forestry has objected to renewed efforts to build a highway connecting Kokee and Haena. The bulldozed scars of the abortive beginnings of this road remain as testimony to disregard of park values and incompetence in protecting them. Plans prepared by the State Parks Division showed the "make-work" highway closed off at the new Kalalau parking area to deny access to vehicles and permit recovery of the native forest. During construction, however, the good intentions of park planners were thwarted by unknown persons who ordered the road left open.

Overgrazing by early ranchers, particularly on the crown-grant lands, was destructive to many thousands of acres. The once forested lands are a depressing example of how uncon-

trolled grazing can destroy a landscape. Overgrazing and serious erosion continue in Kalalau Valley. Only prohibition of grazing and government-financed native tree planting programs can spare Kalalau from the fate of the range lands.

Blackberries were brought into Kokee. Birds carried the seeds far and wide until today, areas of the state park are impenetrable tangles of blackberry bushes climbing hillsides and trees, choking out all native plant life. The State Park Division has had no success in controlling the blackberry at Kokee. Cleared trails grow back and within a year are again impassable. Forestry Division attempts at control by poison spray and bulldozer have doubled the weeds and killed most of the native fern, allowing the blackberry to grow back with renewed vigor.

According to the laws of Hawaii, a state park "is an area which by means of location, natural features, scenic beauty or legendary, historical or scientific interest, possesses distinctive physical, aesthetic, intellectual, creative, or social values." The law further states that "the Board (of Land and Natural Resources) shall preserve the parks and parkways in the State park system in their natural condition so far as may be consistent with their use and safety, and improve them in such manner as to retain to a maximum extent their natural scenic, historic, and wildlife values for the use and enjoyment of the public." The scenic beauty and wilderness values of Kokee State Park, Waimea Canyon State Park, and adjacent State forestry lands and private lands in Kalalau are today in danger of serious injury because these basic provisions for protection of park land have not been respected. By no stretch of the imagination is Kokee-Napali being protected in a manner befitting its stature as one of the greatest national scenic resources in America.

The problems of providing increasing opportunities for recreation and a wilderness experience for larger numbers of visitors and residents, while protecting Hawaii's irreplaceable natural assets, are not being met. Dedication to wilderness values and sufficient funds to support that dedication are apparently lacking.

The Kokee-Napali scenic lands are a unique and valuable asset to the state and the nation. Secretary of the Interior Stewart Udall said, "I consider this one of the most important and significant areas proposed for addition to the National Park system during the nearly five years that I have been Secretary of the Interior. It is one of the crown jewels of the Islands and would be a superb addition to the National Park system."

The Hawaii state park system does not have adequate professional staff or financial resources to carry out a statewide park and recreation program and at the same time provide protection to Kokee-Napali for the enjoyment of Kauai and the nation. The National Park Service does have the staff and resources. To give permanent protection to the scenic beauty of Kauai, to preserve the unique flora and fauna of Alakai Swamp, and to provide for increased recreational opportunities in Kokee-Napali, the Department of the Interior has been asked to bring to Kauai the traditions and high standards of the National Park Service. Many years ago the Park Service came to Haleakala Crater, which was then almost stripped of the silversword, and saved it from extinction by immediately directing that the silversword no longer be picked. A ranger stood by to make sure that the regulation was observed, and the courts punished those

who selfishly picked the golden spectacle of silversword in bloom. The people of Kauai must not wait until the Mokihana disappears before saying in Kokee, "please don't pick the flowers."

On the mainland and on Maui the problem of providing more opportunities for recreation for increasing numbers of visitors while still protecting the parks' irreplaceable natural assets was solved only by building up a tradition of high standards and a corps of highly trained, dedicated personnel who were mindful of the needs of future generations.

A national park on Kauai, run by this corps, would not involve unnecessary restrictions. National Park Service regulations differ little from the rules and regulations of existing state parks. What is involved is enforcement of rules and proper care and maintenance of park country.

Although the advantages of a national park for protection of scenic resources are great and the most important reason for a park's existence, the economic benefit of a national park on Kauai's depressed economy would be enormous. Though the park itself would employ only a few dozen people, there would be considerable additional employment by new hotels and the expanded tourist industry needed to take care of the additional tourist visits and longer stays that would be motivated by the existence of a major national park. In this respect, to compare tiny Haleakala Park with the proposed one hundred-square-mile Kauai National Park is to underestimate Kokee's exciting potential. Kokee would more properly be compared to Grand Teton National Park with its millions of visitors each year.

The National Park Service experience on the mainland is that rapid increases in economic activity follow the declaration of national park status. To quote the National Park Service:

As a matter of record, investigations made in several existing parks have shown commercial enterprises have actually expanded and new enterprises have been developed adjacent to the parks to meet the needs of park visitors. Moreover, adjacent property values have increased, and employment in the region has been observed to rise greatly.

A comparison of Kokee State Park and Hawaii Volcanoes National Park shows that the national park has far greater economic impact on the Islands' economy. During the last five years, Kauai's Kokee State Park was visited by some 500,000 people, and spent about one million dollars on park operations and improvements. In these same years, Volcanoes National Park on Hawaii Island had almost three million visitors and spent over four million dollars on the park. These figures do not include work done by other agencies outside the park boundaries. In 1964 alone, Volcanoes Park had 518,000 visitors—as many as Kokee had in five years. It is estimated that Hawaii Volcanoes National Park, as the major attraction for most visitors to Hawaii Island, especially those on a twenty-four hour visit, may be contributing at least five million dollars a year to the Islands' economy.

The proposed Kauai Park could contribute at least two million dollars a year to the Kauai economy. The park would justify the construction of at least two hotels outside its boundaries to accommodate longer tourist stays in addition to extensive expansion of concession facilities and recreation opportunities for island residents in Kokee.

Further comparison of improvements by the two parks is interesting: in the last five years, Hawaii Volcanoes National Park has improved 30 miles of trails; Kokee State Park has improved less than 10, including trails cleared by the Division of Forestry outside the park boundaries. Volcanoes has constructed 5 miles of new trails; Kokee has constructed none. Volcanoes has constructed a modern natural history museum and visitors' center, staffed by professional naturalists; Kokee has a small, totally inadequate museum with dedicated volunteer attendants, but few resources. Volcanoes has spent more than $20,000 on blackberry eradication; Kokee has spent nothing. Volcanoes has regular patrols to protect the natural scenic beauty, self-guided trails, and naturalist-conducted, interpretive services; Kokee has none.

Kauai's wilderness should have the protection that Volcanoes Park enjoys, and soon, while it remains wilderness, for those who want to discover it and walk on it. For those who choose not to—the tourist standing at Waimea Canyon Lookout, the botanist searching his files in Honolulu; the children scampering the beach sands at Hanalei—there will be, with preservation, the satisfaction of simply knowing it is there forever.

Mamalohoa mountain, Hanalei Bay

Epilogue

... The need is not really for more brains, the need is now for a gentler, a more tolerant people than those who won for us against the ice, the tiger, and the bear. The hand that hefted the ax, out of some old blind allegiance to the past, fondles the machine gun as lovingly. It is a habit man will have to break to survive, but the roots go very deep.

—LOREN EISELEY

We are waking now from the American dream to realize that it was a dream few Americans lived in their waking hours. The history of the New World has turned out to be not so different from that of the Old. The peril that threatens the last of the American wilderness arises not from the reckless dream, but from the same historic forces of rapacity and cruelty that laid waste the land in the Mediterranean Basin, in Arabia, India, and the treeless uplands of China.

The wilderness is there, however, to recall the dream. And lately we have won a reprieve through the advance of scientific understanding.

The frontier of understanding has no limits, and the curse of want and poverty may yet be lifted from the life of our species. That frontier cannot be exploited on the same selfish terms as the frontier that lies behind.

—GERARD PIEL

Unnamed falls, Kalalau Beach pali

Whatever else the word [frontier] means, it has also meant water flowing in clear rivers, a countryside under clean sun or snow, woods, prairies, and mountains of simple loveliness. It is not necessary to think the literature of America a very noble literature in order to recognize the fact that one of its principal occupations has been the celebration of that beauty. Layer after layer of experience or frustration may come between, but at the very base of the American mind an undespoiled country lies open to the sun.

—Bernard DeVoto

The brutal destruction of our landscape is much more than a blow against beauty. Every artist, scientist, and philosopher in the history of mankind has pointed to the laws of nature as his greatest source of inspiration: without the presence of nature, undisturbed, there would have been no Leonardo, no Ruskin, no Nervi, no Frank Lloyd Wright. In destroying our landscape, we are destroying the future of civilization in America.

—Peter Blake

Na Keiki o Na Liwi, Kalalau

Dwarf ohia lehua, Alakai Swamp

Dawn, Waimea Canyon

What is the use of a house if you haven't got a tolerable planet to put it on?

—THOREAU

How little, from the resources unrenewable by Man, cost the things of
        greatest value—
        wild beauty, peace, health and love,
        music and all testaments of spirit!
How simple our basic needs—
        a little food, sun, air, water, shelter, warmth and sleep!
How lightly might this earth bear Man forever!

                                        —NANCY NEWHALL

Ohia lehua and mist